FLORENCE

NEW COMPLETE GUIDEBOOK
TO THE CITY

ß

BECOCCI EDITORE - FIRENZE

HISTORICAL NOTES

Although we do not know when the original town was built, it is known that on the site where the city now lies there was an **Italic** settlement, which was subsequently taken over by the **Etruscans.** During colonisation of the countryside around Fiesole, it became a Roman town under **Silla,** and was known by the augural name of *Florentia.* During the Longobard rule it was the seat of a Duke and then of a Count in the Carolingian era. The city had no particular importance during the Roman Empire or under Barbarian rule. Its very slow growth began only in the tenth and eleventh centuries with the general awakening of the Italian people. It reached full autonomy around 1115 when, on the death of **Countess Matilde** of Tuscany who had ruled the town (and by taking advantage of the conflict between *Papacy* and the *Empire*), it succeeded in proclaiming itself a free Commune, fighting against the feudal lords, and established supremacy over the nearby towns.

The wealthy noble class soon had the upper hand in ruling the *Comune.* This class was made up partly of the richest merchants and the clergy, but mostly of noble families perennially fighting against each other for supremacy. The murder of **Buondelmonte dei Buondelmonti** (Easter 1215) divided the nobility into two factions: the **Amidei** and **Uberti** and the **Buondelmonti** and **Donati.** Under the names of *Ghibellines* and *Guelphs*, they fought desperately for nearly a century. Despite fighting among the factions, the city prospered and gained military power; Pisa, Pistoia, Volterra and Arezzo came under its rule.

After the victory of **Monteaperti** (1260), the Ghibellines, who had been thrown out of the city ten years earlier, returned with **Farinata**

2

degli Uberti at their head. But after the fall of the Swabians, the Guelph party, supported by the popular masses, triumphed once more (1267).

Guelph Florence defeated Siena in the Battle of **Colle Val d'Elsa** (1269) and **Arezzo** at **Campaldino** (1289), whilst its rival **Pisa** was defeated by the Genoese in the **Meloria** naval battle (1284). Florence supremacy was thus asserted over most of **Tuscany.**

Towards the end of thirteenth century the population, with the publication of the *Ordinamenti di Giustizia* by **Giano della Bella** (1293), rebelled against the return of the feudal lords. These "Ordinamenti" (Orders) entrusted the government to the Trade Guilds which were mainly represented by the seven *Major Arts*, made up of the "popolo grasso" (nobles and rich merchants).

In 1300 the Guelphs split into *Bianchi* and *Neri*, led respectively by the **Cerchi** and the **Donati**. The Priors (including **Dante**) exiled the leaders of the two factions, but the Neri (Blacks) supported by **Charles of Valois** (sent to their aid by **Boniface VIII**) succeeded in gaining the upper hand and exiled the Bianchi (Whites) and then **Dante Alighieri** himself (1302).

In 1342 a French adventurer, **Gautier di Brienne**, Duke of Athens, obtained the signory of Florence for life, but the Florentines grew tired of his bad government and threw him out of the city in 1343, thus gaining their freedom again. To face the dangers of Restoration of the *Papal State*, undertaken by Cardinal **Albornoz**, Florence entered into war with Pope **Gregory XI** (the "Eight Saints" War 1375-78), and went through a disastrous economic and political crisis which led to the **Ciompi** revolt (1378). The "popolo minuto" (small entrepreneurs and workers), under the severe corporative control of the Guilds, obtained the right to represent

3

itself, implementing a real demagogic legislation. The reaction of the upper middle class was immediate: they overthrew the democratic government and abolished the New Guilds (1382). Florence came under the rule of the richest families (**Albizi, Capponi, Uzzano**). Although the new rule had the merit of saving the independence of the Commune from the efforts of supremacy of **Gian Galeazzo Visconti** (1390)-1402), and **Ladislao,** King of Naples (1409-1414), in the long run it divided itself just the same into two opposing groups: an aristocratic faction and a popular faction.

The rich and ambitious family of the **Medici** with **Cosimo the Elder**, having defeated the **Albizi** with the help of the people, managed to gain control of the city (1434), restoring, if not yet by name, the *Signoria* regime. After **Cosimo** (1434-64) the supremacy of the Medicis continued with the weak **Piero il Gottoso** (Piero the Gouty) (1464-69), who seemed to endanger the family's destiny; his son **Lorenzo**, however, who was subsequently to be known as the **Magnificent** (1449-92), managed to defeat the *Pazzi conspiracy* (1478) and consolidate his own power; by making an alliance with Naples and Milan, he also created a political balance to safeguard the freedom of the "Italian States". When **Lorenzo** died at the age of forty, his son **Piero** was not able to continue his father's work. **Charles VIII** took advantage of Piero's inability to govern and occupied Florence in 1494. The Florentines, encouraged by the preaching of the Dominican friar **Girolamo Savonarola**, managed to throw him out and proclaimed the *Republic* (1494-1512). The vigour of Savonarola's religious reform was not well tolerated by Pope **Alexander VI Borgia**. Savonarola was hanged in *Piazza della Signoria* on 23rd May 1498. The **Medici**, having returned to Florence, strengthened their power by placing two members of their family on the pontifical throne (**Leo X** and **Clement VII**). The *Sack of Rome* (1527) was a second blow to the Medici family who once again lost its power. It was the beginning of the *Second Republic* (1527-1530), but the Peace of Barcellona between the Pope and the Emperor (1529) marked its end. In fact, the heroic resistance of the citizens against the siege of the Imperial troops, commanded by

Cofer with the procession of St. John, detail.

4

15th century map of Florence, detail.

Filiberto d'Orange and the ability of **Francesco Ferrucci**, only served to make the end of the Florentine's freedom (1530) more glorious. The Medici family, with **Alexander** who had earned the title of Duke (1532) and **Cosimo I** with the title of *Grand-Duke* (1569), officially asserted its power and with the *conquest of Siena* (1555) expanded the frontiers of its *State* over which the family ruled uncontested until 1737 when, with **Gian Gastone**, the last of the Medicis, the family became extinct and the **Grand Duchy** passed to **Francis Stephan**, Duke of **Lorraine,** and husband of **Maria Teresa of Hapsburg**, then *Empress of Austria*. Tuscany therefore remained closely tied to the house of *Hapsburg-Lorraine* until the death of **Francis Stephan** in 1785 when, with the appointment of his second son **Peter Leopold** as Grand Duke, Florence once again gained a certain autonomy; this allowed it to carry out some important illuministic reforms around the second half of the eighteenth century. Except for a very short period of French rule (1799-1815), Tuscany remained under the rule of the Hapsburg-Lorraine family up to 1860 when with a plebiscite it became part of the reign of **Victor Emmanuel II.** With the unification of Italy, Florence became capital of the new *Kingdom* (1865-1871). It was during this period that the **Savoy** dynasty demolished (1887) the historical and ancient quarter of the old market making way for the present *Piazza della Repubblica*, which fits in rather badly with the rest of the city where the Medieval and Renaissance atmosphere is still preserved.

During the second world war Florence was the scene of fighting between the partisans and German troops and suffered heavy damage especially in the oldest parts of the city on both sides of *Ponte Vecchio*, the only bridge over the **Arno** spared by the Germans in August 1944. Other serious damage was suffered in the old part of the city during the flood of 4th November 1966.

FIRST ITINERARY

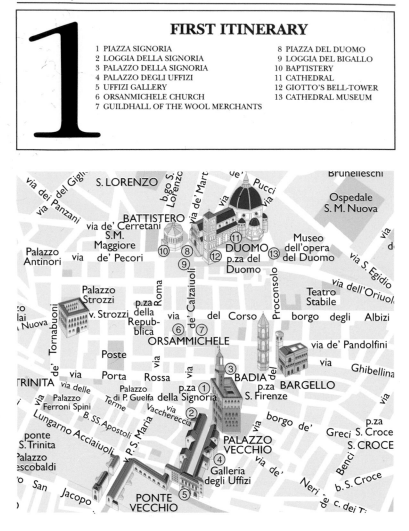

1 PIAZZA SIGNORIA
2 LOGGIA DELLA SIGNORIA
3 PALAZZO DELLA SIGNORIA
4 PALAZZO DEGLI UFFIZI
5 UFFIZI GALLERY
6 ORSANMICHELE CHURCH
7 GUILDHALL OF THE WOOL MERCHANTS

8 PIAZZA DEL DUOMO
9 LOGGIA DEL BIGALLO
10 BAPTISTERY
11 CATHEDRAL
12 GIOTTO'S BELL-TOWER
13 CATHEDRAL MUSEUM

1 **PIAZZA DELLA SIGNORIA** - Built around the end of the thirteenth century as a symmetrical contrast to the city's religious centre, *Piazza della Signoria* was enlarged through demolition of the tower-houses of the Uberti, Foraboschi and other powerful Ghibelline families. Right from Medieval times, Piazza della Signoria has always been the civic centre of Florentine life. Although some original buildings (the *Loggia dei Pisani* and the *Church of St Cecilia*) and the ancient brick paving, which gave it greater unity of style, have now disappeared, it remains in all its aspects a square of incomparable beauty and elegance. Dominated by the fourteenth-century *Palazzo della Signoria* with its high crenellated tower, it is surrounded by other important buildings: the *Loggia della Signoria* and the *Palazzo degli Uffizi* on the south side, the sixteenth-century *Palazzo degli Uguccioni* on the north side and the *Palazzo del Tribunale di Mercanzia* (circa 1359) on the east side. The *Palazzo delle Assicurazioni Generali* on the west side of the square, a cold imitation of Renaissance style, was built by Landi in

Piazza della Signoria.

The "Biancone" by Ammannati.

1871. The square, where public tournaments and feasts took place between 1400 and 1500, was transformed almost into an open-air museum in the sixteenth century by the addition of several statues. From left to right one can admire: *the bronze equestrian* statue of **Great Duke Cosimo I**, a late work of **Giambologna** (1594); the large and monumental ***Ammannati*** *Fountain* (1575), ironically called

7

"Biancone" because of the remarkable difference between the ugly and heavy central statue of Neptune and the slender figures of the satyrs and nymphs leaning on the waved border of the fountain. In front of the fountain, almost at the centre of the square, a granite disc commemorates the place where Savonarola and his faithful followers, Frà Domenico and Frà Silvestro, were hanged and burned (23rd May 1498). On the steps of Palazzo della Signoria from left to right: a copy of the *Marzocco*, i.e. a lion with the Florentine lily, (the original of which is preserved in the Bargello) and a copy of the group of *Judith and Holofernes* (the original is in the Piazza della Signoria Museum), outstanding works by **Donatello** (1460 circa), a copy of the famous *David* by **Michelangelo,** the original of which is in the Academy Gallery, and the marble group of *Hercules and Cacus* by **Baccio Bandinelli** (1536).

In the same square, at no. 5, one can visit the collection of **Alberto della Ragione**, donated to the city of Florence in 1970. This important *collection of Italian contemporary art* includes works by well-known painters and sculptors of our time, as for example, Carrà, De Chirico, De Pisis, Guttuso, Morandi, Fontana and Manzù.

2 **LOGGIA DELLA SIGNORIA** - The *Loggia della Signoria* or *dei Priori*, (known also as the *Loggia dell'Orcagna* because of a drawing allegedly by this artist, or *Loggia dei Lanzi*, because during the rule of Grand Duke Cosimo I a Lantzchnecht Guard was billeted there), was built by **Benci di Cione** and **Simone Talenti** between 1376 and 1382. Although both private and public loggias already existed in Florence, the Signoria wanted to build one for itself, large and stately, from which the authorities could present themselves to the people, giving greater emphasis to the most important events of municipal life: and it was here, in fact, that Priors and Gonfaloniers were instated, embassies were received and edicts were issued.

From an architectural point of view the loggia is one of the best examples of late fourteenth-century Florentine Gothic style. It is composed of wide arches, supported by clustered columns, covered by cross vaults and horizontally crowned by small arched porches which support the elegant triple parapet of the terrace. It is decorated at the top with the coats-of-arms of the Republic and

Piazza della Signoria: The Loggia of the Lanzi.

Giambologna: The Rape of the Sabine.   *Cellini: Perseus.*

lobed plaques on the spandrels, to a design by **Agnolo Gaddi**, and symbolises the theological and cardinal virtues. The clear and balanced decoration and structure expresses such a new concept that it almost infringes the Gothic style. On the entrance staircase there are *two lions* (the lion, like the lily was a symbol of the Republic), the one on the right in classical style, the one on the left in sixteenth-century style.

The sculptures now exhibited were placed here after the fall of the Republic when the loggia had lost its original political and social use. Under the arch on the right is the famous marble group of the *Rape of the Sabines*, the work of **Giambologna** (1583), which the artist initially called *The Three Ages*. Under the left arch stands the famous *Perseus* (1554), a bronze masterpiece by **Benvenuto Cellini**, who recalls its casting in one of the most beautiful pages of *Vita*. In this work the careful analysis of detail, rendered with the sensibility of a goldsmith, lends a sense of unity.

In the central part of the loggia, from right to left, *Hercules* and the *Centaur* by **Giambologna** (1599), *Menelaus* or *Ajax supporting the body of Patroclus,* a Hellenistic copy of the Greek original, and the *Rape of Polyxena* by **Pio Fedi** (1866); standing against the back wall are six antique statues of Roman matrons.

PALAZZO DELLA SIGNORIA - In 1293, after the political success **3** of the guilds, the new Priors wanted to build a monument which would become the most important civic monument in Florence, the *Palazzo dei Priori*, seat of the Signoria, later called *Palazzo Vecchio*. According to tradition, the central nucleus of the building was

Palazzo Vecchio.

erected by **Arnolfo di Cambio** between 1299 and 1304. It has the appearance of a fortress, topped by a huge open gallery, from which rises the slender tower known as the ***Arnolfo tower*** and which repeats in the belfry the design of the top of the palace. The rusticated walls are horizontally scanned by slender cornices and two rows of elegant ogival mullioned windows; this is the only concession to Gothic taste, which gives a sense of harmony and measured proportion to the Palace. It was subsequently enlarged - by **Vasari,** in the sixteenth century and by **Buontalenti,** in the seventeenth century. Palazzo Vecchio, after having been the seat of the town authorities, became the home of the Medici family. Later it was the seat of the provisional governments (1848-49) and 1859-60), and when Florence was the capital of Italy from 1865 to 1871 it housed the Chamber of Deputies and the Foreign Ministry. It has been the seat of the municipal authorities since 1872.

Courtyard - In 1470 **Michelozzo** gave a Renaissance look to the courtyard, but the decoration of the columns with gold stuccoes, the vault of the portico with grotesque figures and the walls painted with views of principal Austrian cities are the work of **Vasari,** realised for the marriage of Francis I de' Medici with Jane of Austria. At the centre of the very pretty *fountain* in porphyry is a winged putto in bronze, a copy of the original by **Andrea del Verrocchio** (1476) housed in the Palace Museum. On the left side of the portico is the entrance to the ***Sala d'Arme*** (Weapons

10

Palazzo Vecchio: The courtyard by Michelozzo.

Room), the only part of the palace which still maintains Arnolfian architectural characteristics. From the Courtyard the monumental double *Vasarian Staircase* leads to the first floor.

Salone dei Cinquecento (Hall of the Five Hundred) - The work of **Simone del Pollaiolo**, also known as the **Cronaca** (1495), it is 53 metres long and 22 metres wide. This hall was originally intended for meetings of the People's General Council. In 1848 it became the seat of the Tuscan parliament. It was here that the annexation of Tuscany to the Kingdom of Italy was proclaimed in 1860; from 1865 to 1871, when Florence was the capital, it was the seat of the Chamber of Deputies. Cosimo I however commissioned **Vasari** to convert it into a reception hall (1563-65) for dancing and public feasts. The huge frescoes on the walls and ceiling exalting Cosimo I and his family are works of **Vasari** and his assistants. A set of sculptures is arranged along the walls; the first to the left of the entrance *Florence conquering Pisa* is a plaster model by **Giambologna**; the six marble groups representing the *Labours of Hercules* were sculptured by **Vincenzo de' Rossi**.
On the wall opposite the entrance is the *Genius of Victory* by **Michelangelo** (1534), which he had intended for the tomb of Pope

The great Hall of the 500.

Vasari: Capture of the Town of Pisa, detail.

Vasari: Epilogue of the war of Siena, detail.

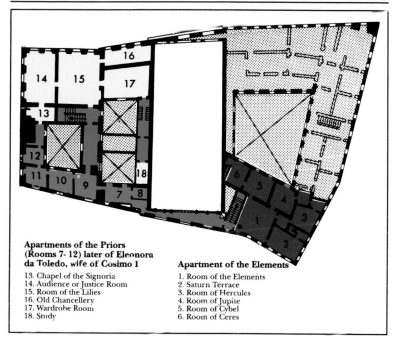

Apartments of the Priors
(Rooms 7- 12) later of Eleonora
da Toledo, wife of Cosimo I

13. Chapel of the Signoria
14. Audience or Justice Room
15. Room of the Lilies
16. Old Chancellery
17. Wardrobe Room
18. Study

Apartment of the Elements

1. Room of the Elements
2. Saturn Terrace
3. Room of Hercules
4. Room of Jupite
5. Room of Cybel
6. Room of Ceres

Julius II; on the opposite side (raised) known as *dell'Udienza*, in the central niche is a statue of *Leo X* by Bandinelli. A hall on the left leads to the **Sala dei Dugento**, named after the number of members of the Council of the Republic and now seat of the Municipal Authorities; the ornate *coffered ceiling* is the work of **Benedetto** and **Giuliano da Maiano** (1477).

Study of Francis I - From the *Salone dei Cinquecento* one enters the studiolo of Francis I, beautifully decorated by **Vasari** (1570-72) and other late sixteenth-century mannerists. It was built as a place of study and meditation by the eccentric Prince, a scholar of Nature's mystery and an expert in alchemy.

In the barrel vault the allegories of Prometheus and the elements are by Poppi, whilst the tondos with the *portraits* of *Cosimo I* and *Eleanor of Toledo* are by **Bronzino.**

The paintings on the partitions in the upper fillets of the walls illustrate the works of Man in relation to the various elements; those on the lower doors of the wardrobes are mythological, alchemical and divinatory episodes. In the niches there are elegant bronze statues of mythological divinities.

Apartments of Leo X - Access to these apartments is from the *Salone dei Cinquecento*. It comprises six rooms, decorated by **Vasari** and his assistants (1560) with frescoes which celebrate the Medici family. In the *Room of Leo X,* to the left of the chimney, is the *Chapel* with a copy of the Madonna dell'Impannata, by Raphael; the original is now in the Palatine Gallery; there follow: The *Room of Clement VII* with frescoes showing a panoramic view of the S*iege of Florence of 1529-30,* a work of particular historical interest; the *Room of Giovanni delle Bande Nere*, the *Room of Cosimo I*, the *Room of Lorenzo the Magnificent* and the *Room of Cosimo the Elder*, all decorated with portraits and episodes of the lives of the people to whom they are

Vasari and Stradano: The siege of Florence (Clemente VII's room).

Michelangelo: Genius of Victory.   *Vincenzo de' Rossi: Hercules and Diomedes.*

14

Small studio of Francis I° de' Medici.

The Hall of Leo X.

dedicated. Apart from the first, they are today used by the Municipal Authorities as the mayor's private offices.

From the Room of Leo X a door opens on to the staircase which leads to the second floor. On the landing is the fresco of the *Feast of St John*, by **Stradano** with an interesting night view of Piazza della Signoria.

Apartment of the Elements - Made up of five rooms built by **Battista del Tasso** in 1550 and decorated by **Vasari** and his assistants between 1556 and 1566. The first is known as the *Room of the Elements* because of the allegorical frescoes by Vasari and Doceno of the four elements: earth, air, water and fire. The others are: the *Room of Hercules*, with a representation of the Labours of Hercules, also by Doceno; the *Room of Jupiter*, with Jupiter's childhood depicted on the ceiling and a sixteenth-century Florentine tapestry executed from cartoons by Stradano; between these two, in the small Loggia of Juno, today walled up, is the original of the bronze *Winged Putto* by **Verrocchio**; the *Room of Cybele* has the Triumph of Cybele and the Four Seasons on the ceiling and an eighteenth-century Florentine tapestry and the *Room of Ceres* has a sixteenth-century Florentine tapestry and works by Vasari and Doceno. From

The Priori Chapel.

Hall of the Elements.

the Room of the Elements one enters the ***Loggia of Saturn*** where the bronze *Devil* by **Giambologna** is preserved; from here one can enjoy a splendid view of the city.

Apartments of Eleonora di Toledo - This was at one time the Apartment of the Priors. It consists of the ***Green Room,*** decorated with works by **Ridolfo del Ghirlandaio**; the *Chapel of Eleonora*, with frescoes by **Bronzino** showing *Stories of Moses*; the *Room of the Sabines*, frequented by the ladies of the court, with portraits of members of the Medici family; the *Room of Esther*, or the Dining room, with a fifteenth-century marble wash-basin and precious Florentine tapestries; the *Room of Penelope* with frescoes in the style of Botticelli; the *Room of the Gualdrada* with frescoes on the wall representing tales of the "beautiful Gualdrada" a virtuous damsel, to whom Dante makes reference in (*Inferno*, Canto XV), commissioned by Cosimo I to honour his wife's faithfulness; the frieze in this room shows *views of squares* in sixteenth-century Florence.

One now reaches the *Chapel of the Signoria*, dedicated to Saint Bernard with frescoes by **Ridolfo del Ghirlandaio** of 1514 (the *Annunciation*), whilst the panel above the altar, *Madonna with Child, St Elizabeth and St John*, is the work of **Mariano da Pescia**. *The Audience Hall*: built by **Benedetto da Maiano** (1475-81) who, with his brother **Giuliano**, also created the lovely white marble portal surmounted by the *statue of Justice* (1478); **Giuliano** also produced the priceless octagonal coffered ceiling, while the frescoes on the walls, representing *tales of Camillo*, are the work of Salviati (1560).

Room of the Lilies - This was also built by **Benedetto da Maiano**, whilst the beautiful gilded wood ceiling is the work by **Giuliano da Maiano**; the *marble portal* leading into the Audience Hall is by B. da Maiano (1481) and is quite remarkable, with its wooden shutters representing Dante and Petrarch, the work of Francione and G. da Maiano. On the left is the original of **Donatello**'s masterpiece *Judith and Holofernes* (1460 circa) which, after skilful restoration work, can now be admired in all its splendour.

Chancellery - This was used as an office by **Niccolò Machiavelli** when he was secretary of the Florentine Republic (1498-1512); he is represented here in a portrait by **Santi di Tito** and in a marble bust. An item of great interest in this room is the fourteenth-century mullioned window with two lights, which was once at the northern corner of the rear façade of the Palace, and the relief representing

Hall of the Lilies.

18

Donatello: Judith and Olofernes, detail (Hall of the Lilies).

St George and the Dragon, which comes from the city gate of the same name, by **Arnolfo di Cambio**.

Wardrobe Room - Here the Medicis kept their precious objects. Of particular interest are the *Globe* by **Ignazio Danti** (1567) and the 53 *maps* painted by Danti himself and by **Stefano Buonsignori**, showing all the parts of the world that were known in the sixteenth century. Coming down towards the **Mezzanine Apartments** one arrives at the five rooms where the **Loeser collection** is exhibited; this collection was offered to the Florence Municipality by the art critic Charles Loeser (1928) and contains paintings and sculptures of the Tuscan school of the fourteenth to the sixteenth century. Still other rooms house works of remarkable quality, recovered from abroad after the war. Lastly, there is the *Tower*, 94 metres high, from where one can enjoy a splendid view. An educational tour can be reserved for children in the Children's Museum.

PALAZZO DEGLI UFFIZI - A late Renaissance masterpiece of town 4 planning and architecture by **Vasari**. The *Palazzo degli Uffizi* was begun in 1560 and completed in 1580 by **Alfonso Parigi** and **Bernardo Buontalenti** who followed the original design. It was commissioned by Grand Duke Cosimo I to house the public offices (uffizi) in the same building. Through alterations to the historical centre of Florence, **Vasari** was able to insert, between Palazzo Vecchio and the Loggia della Signoria, the long *arcade* of the Uffizi Palace. The result is a beautiful view which ends with a Loggia that looks out over the River Arno. A series of statues representing the most famous Tuscan personalities was placed in the niches of the huge arcade columns in the nineteenth century. The famous *Corridoio Vasariano* (Vasari Corridor) passes over Ponte Vecchio, and joins up with the Pitti Palace, thus creating a private and direct link between the home of the Grand Duke and Parliament. Since 1973 it has housed, besides a series of seventeenth and eighteenth-

View of the Piazzale of the Uffizi.

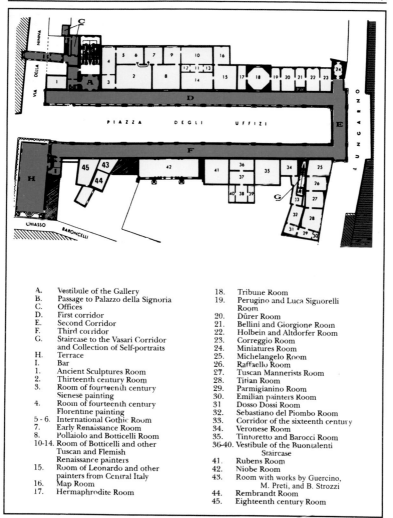

A.	Vestibule of the Gallery	18.	Tribune Room
B.	Passage to Palazzo della Signoria	19.	Perugino and Luca Signorelli Room
C.	Offices	20.	Dürer Room
D.	First corridor	21.	Bellini and Giorgione Room
E.	Second Corridor	22.	Holbein and Altdorfer Room
F.	Third corridor	23.	Correggio Room
G.	Staircase to the Vasari Corridor and Collection of Self-portraits	24.	Miniatures Room
H.	Terrace	25.	Michelangelo Room
I.	Bar	26.	Raffaello Room
1.	Ancient Sculptures Room	27.	Tuscan Mannerists Room
2.	Thirteenth century Room	28.	Titian Room
3.	Room of fourteenth century Sienese painting	29.	Parmigianino Room
4.	Room of fourteenth century Florentine painting	30.	Emilian painters Room
		31	Dosso Dossi Room
5 - 6.	International Gothic Room	32.	Sebastiano del Piombo Room
7.	Early Renaissance Room	33.	Corridor of the sixteenth century
8.	Pollaiolo and Botticelli Room	34.	Veronese Room
10-14.	Room of Botticelli and other Tuscan and Flemish Renaissance painters	35.	Tintoretto and Barocci Room
		36-40.	Vestibule of the Buontalenti Staircase
15.	Room of Leonardo and other painters from Central Italy	41.	Rubens Room
		42.	Niobe Room
16.	Map Room	43.	Room with works by Guercino, M. Preti, and B. Strozzi
17.	Hermaphrodite Room	44.	Rembrandt Room
		45.	Eighteenth century Room

century paintings, the famous *Collection of Self-portraits* by Italian and foreign artists, which are grouped according to school and nationality. Amongst these self-portraits, nearly always donated to the city by the artists themselves, it is worth recalling the portraits of the Italian painters Vasari, Andrea del Sarto, Raphael, the Carraccis, Bernini, Salvator Rosa, Canova and Fattori and the foreign artists Rubens, Rembrandt, Velàzquez, Corot, Delacroix, Ingres, Böcklin and Ensor, right up to the most recent gift from Chagall.

UFFIZI GALLERY - This is one of the most important artistic collections in the world. It was begun by **Francis I de' Medici** who put into practice the plans of **Cosimo I**, gathering together all the family's collections on the second floor of the palace. The collection was enriched in particular by **Ferdinand I**, who transferred various sculptures from the Medici Villa in Rome to the Uffizi. Thanks to the inheritance of **Cardinal Leopold** and to the **5**

21

patronage of **Cosimo II** and **Peter Leopold of Lorraine**, the artistic patrimony became more and more substantial. From the beginning of the nineteenth century onwards it has concentrated mainly on paintings, the collection of sculptures and tapestries serving only for decorative purposes.

Contini Bonacossi Collection - The gallery on the corner of Via Lambertesca and Chiasso Baroncelli contains the Contini Bonacossi collection. Donated to the government in 1969, it includes important paintings and sculptures from the Italian school. Contact the superintendency to schedule a visit.

Entrance Hall - Here there is a marble group of Mars and Venus, a Roman copy of a Hellenistic original. From this room one enters what remains of the ancient Romanesque church of *San Piero Scheraggio* (eleventh century), which was demolished to build a Palace.
These rooms contain paintings and detached frescoes including the famous cycle of *portraits of famous personages*, a work by **Andrea del Castagno** of mid fifteenth century; on the right hand wall is the Battle of St Martin by Corrado Cagli (1936). On leaving, on the left, is **Botticelli**'s priceless fresco of the Annunciation, which comes from the church of San Martino alla Scala.

Vestibule - Two columns with frescoes, one of which depicting St Francis, again recall the original church of San Piero Scheraggio; there is also a sculpture in bronze by **Giorgio De Chirico**, the *Archaeologists*, donated by the artist, and a large portrait of the Palatine Electress, Anna Maria Ludovica, who presented the **Medicean Collections** to Florence.
The *Vasari Staircase*, on which ancient sculptures are exhibited, leads to the *Cabinet of Drawings and Prints* by Italian and foreign artists, one of the richest collections in the world and to a special *Library* and a *Photographic Archive*. Climbing the Great Staircase one reaches the second floor.

Gallery Vestibule (A) - With a display of ancient statues

First Gallery (D) - The ceiling of the long and extremely bright upper lodge, with its huge windows, is decorated with freely-inspired *grotesques* and executed by Florentine artists of the second half of the sixteenth century.
Displayed along the top of the walls is a *collection of portraits of famous personages*. All along the Loggia are exhibited busts, sarcophagi and ancient Roman, Greek and Hellenistic statues. Worthy of note, at the beginning of the north side, is the group of *Hercules killing the Centaur*, a Roman copy of the famous Greek original.

Room I - Houses some pieces of classic sculpture, including the Hellenistic alto-rilievo of the *Sitting Wayfarer*, the Roman copy of the Hellenistic original of the *Torso of Dorifore* and the *Bust of Cicero*.

Room II - Dedicated to **Giotto** (1267 circa-1337) and to the Tuscan Primitives. It houses works of the thirteenth century Lucca, Pisan, Sienese and Florentine schools.
The most important of these are: The *Madonna in Majesty* by **Cimabue** (1280-85), from the High Altar of the church of Santa Trinità, a fundamental work showing the artist's maturity; The *Madonna Enthroned with Child, Angels and Saints* by **Giotto,** painted for the All Saints Church (1305-10); *The Madonna Enthroned with Child and Angels* by **Duccio di Buoninsegna**, leader of the Sienese school, which comes from the Rucellai Chapel in Santa Maria Novella (circa 1985); a *Crucifix* and *Scenes from the life of Christ* from the Lucca school of the thirteenth century; *a Crucifix and Stories of*

Giotto: Maestà of Ognissanti.

the Passion from the Pisan School of the thirteenth century; the *Polyptych of Badia* by **Giotto.**

Room III - Dedicated to the Sienese School of the fourteenth century. **Simone Martini**: *Annunciation* (1333), work of the highest pictorial quality with the sinuous rhythm of its Gothic line and its exquisite chromatic elegance. Amongst the works of **Ambrogio Lorenzetti**: *Presentation of Jesus at the Temple* (1342) and *Scenes from the Life of St Nicholas of Bari;* amongst the works of **Piero Lorenzetti**: *Scenes from the Life of Sacred Humility* (1341) and *Madonna in Glory.*

Room IV - Dedicated to the Florentine school of the fourteenth century and in particular to that of Giotto, one can admire *St Cecilia*

Simone Martini: The Annunciation, detail.

and Scenes from her life, by the so-called **Master of St Cecilia**; *Madonna with child and angels* (1355) by **Taddeo Gaddi**; *Deposition* by **Giottino**; *Madonna in Glory* (1334) by **Bernardo Daddi**; *St Matthew and Episodes from his life* by **Andrea Orcagna** and **Jacopo di Cione**.

Rooms V - VI - Both rooms are devoted to Florentine and International Gothic, so called because of its widespread use throughout the courts of Europe. The paintings shown include: *The Coronation of the Virgin* and *Adoration of the Magi* (1420) by **Lorenzo Monaco**; *Thebaid* by **Gherardo Starnina**; *Madonna with Child and Sts. Peter, Paul, Thomas Aquinas and Dominic,* by **Giovanni di Paolo**; *Crucifixion* by **Agnolo Gaddi**; *Madonna with Child* by **Jacopo Bellini** and the *Adoration of the Magi* (1423) by **Gentile da Fabriano.**

Room VII - This room is dedicated to the early fifteenth century Tuscan painters. The paintings exhibited are: *The Battle of San Romano,* painted around 1456 by **Paolo Uccello** (of the three famous battles by this artist, this is the central panel; of the other two, one is in the Louvre Museum and the other in the National Gallery, London); the portraits of *Federico Montefeltro, Duke of Urbino* and his wife *Battista Sforza* (on the back of both are the allegorical *Triumphs* of the Duke and Duchess), a work by **Piero della Francesca** (1465-66); *Madonna with child and St Anne* (1420-24) by **Masaccio** and **Masolino**; *Madonna with Child and Saints* (circa 1445) by **Domenico Veneziano**; *Madonna with Child,* a late work of **Beato Angelico**; *Coronation of the Virgin* (1430-35) by the same artist.

Room VIII - Dedicated to **Filippo Lippi** and his pupils. Amongst the works of this master: *Coronation of the Virgin, Madonna Enthroned with Child and Saints, Adoration of the Child with St Bernard, Adoration of the Child with St Ilarione,* the very well-known *Madonna with Child and two*

Paolo Uccello: The Battle of S. Romano, detail.

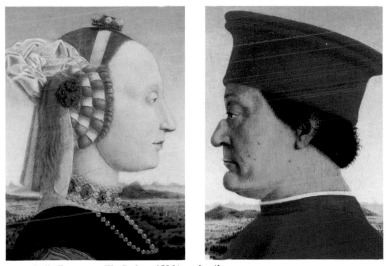

Piero Della Francesca: The Dukes of Urbino, detail.

Angels, work of his full maturity, which dates back to 1465. In addition, *Annunciation* by **Alessio Baldovinetti**; *Stories of St Benedict* by **Neroccio di Bartolomeo Landi** and *St Vincent, St James and St Eustace* by **Antonio** and **Piero del Pollaiolo.**

Room IX - Dedicated to **Antonio** and **Pietro del Pollaiolo.** In this room one can admire: *Portrait of a Lady*, ascribed to Piero della Francesca, Domenico Veneziano and Verrocchio and now to A. del Pollaiolo; *Portrait of Galeazzo Maria Sforza* by P. del Pollaiolo on a drawing allegedly by his brother Antonio; the small paintings of *Hercules and Anteo* and *Hercules and Hydra*, some of the finest works of A. del Pollaiolo; *Six Virtues*, painted in 1470 by P. del Pollaiolo for the Trade Tribunal.
Besides these, the Room also houses works by **Sandro Botticelli** painted in his youth, including: *The Return of Judith from Holofernes'*

25

Masaccio and Masolino: Madonna and St Anne Metterza.

camp, the *Discovery of the Murder of Holofernes,* and the *Fortress,* which completes the Pollaiolo series of Virtues.

Room X - XI - XII - XIII - XIV - This has recently been transformed into one huge room where masterpieces by **Sandro Botticelli** (1445-1510) and the works of Tuscan and Flemish painters of the late fifteenth century are collected together. Amongst paintings by Botticelli, the artist who represented the highest ideals of fifteenth century Medicean Florence, thus creating a new sense of beauty, one can admire: *Allegory of Spring* (1477-78) which evokes the classical myth of Lucrezio and Poliziano; *The Birth of Venus,* painted around 1486, was also inspired by Poliziano's verses; the *Madonna of the Pomegranate,* with its beautiful original frame; the *Magnificat Madonna, Annunciation, Adoration of the Magi, Pallas and the Centaur, Madonna of St Barnaba* and *Allegory of Calumny,* a fundamental work of the later period (1494).

Of particular interest in the same room are: *The Portinari Triptych,* a masterpiece of **Hugo Van Der Goes** (1476-78); *Self-portrait, Adoration of the Magi, Madonna degli Otto* by **Filippino Lippi**; *Adoration of the Magi* by **Domenico del Ghirlandaio**; *Deposition* by **Roger Van Der**

Filippo Lippi: Madonna with Child and two Angels.

Weyden; *Portrait of an Unknown man* and *Portrait of Benedetto Portinari* by **Hans Memling.**

Room XV - Dedicated to the major Umbrian painters, to Tuscan painters of the second half of the fifteenth century and to **Leonardo** (1452-1519). Works by **Luca Signorelli**: *The Holy Family, Crucifix* and *Mary Magdalen*; by **Perugino**: *Pieta, Madonna with Child and two Saints*; by **Lorenzo di Credi**: *Adoration of the Shepherds*; by **Piero di Cosimo**: *the Incarnation.*

Also displayed is the famous B*aptism of Christ* by **Verrocchio** (circa 1470) where in the figure of the angel seen in profile and in the landscape, the hand of his very young pupil, Leonardo, is recognisable. In the same room is the splendid Annunciation, another work by the young **Leonardo** (circa 1475) and the famous *Adoration of the Magi* (1481), a work which though unfinished can be considered his first great masterpiece.

Room XVI - Known also as the *Map Room* because of the maps of Tuscany frescoed on the walls by the cartographer **Stefano Buonsignori** in 1589. The room also houses portraits by **Memling.**

27

Hugo Van Der Goes: Adoration of the Shepherds - Triptych Portinari, detail.

Ghirlandaio: Madonna and Child enthroned with saints.

28

Botticelli: The retour of Judith, detail.

Room XVII - Also called the ***Sleeping Hermaphrodite Room,*** from the Roman copy of the Hellenistic original. On the walls, in the false porphyry niches, stand statues and small bronzes which can be dated between the sixteenth and eighteenth centuries, with the marble group of *Cupid and Psyche*, a copy of the Hellenistic original, and the triptych by **Andrea Mantegna** with the *Adoration of the Shepherds*, the *Circumcision* and the *Ascension.*

Room XVIII - Known also as the ***Tribune,*** it was built by **Buontalenti** in the second half of the sixteenth century and decorated by **Poccetti**; it is a fine example of late sixteenth-century mannerist taste. The sculptures include: in the centre, the famous *Medici Venus* of the classical period, a copy of the praxitelic original of IV-III century BC., the *Little Apollo,* which also derives from praxitelic art; the *Knife-grinder,* the only existing copy of an original by the Pergamene School, the *Dancing Faun* copy of the Hellenistic original of the III century BC, the *Wrestlers,* also a Hellenistic copy of an original from the Pergamene School. Among the paintings: a series of portraits painted by well-known sixteenth-century Florentine mannerists such as **Pontormo** (*Cosimo the Elder*), **Bronzino** (*Lucrezia Panciatichi* and *Eleonora da Toledo*), **Vasari** (*Lorenzo the Magnificent*). The painting of *San Giovannino* by **Raphael** has been here since 1589.

Room XIX - Dedicated to **Perugino** and **Luca Signorelli**. Works by Perugino include: *Portrait of Don Biagio Milanesi, Portrait of*

Botticelli.
Above left: Allegory of the Spring.
Below left: The Birth of Venus.
Above: Allegory of the Spring, detail.

Albrecht Dürer: Adoration of the Magi, detail.

Leonardo: The Annunciation, detail.

Baldassarre Vallombrosano and *Portrait of Francesco delle Opere,* by Signorelli: *The Holy Family and Madonna with Child,* another of his masterpieces; In addition, *Portrait of Evangelista Scappi,* work of Francesco Francia.

Room XX - Dedicated to **Dürer,** great personage of the German Renaissance.
The exhibited works include: *Portrait of Father,* a work of his youth; *Adoration of the Magi,* one of his masterpieces; *St Philip and St James.* Also worthy of particular attention in the same room are two paintings by **Lukas Cranach:** *St George* and *Portrait of Luther.*

Room XXI - Dedicated to fifteenth-century Venetian painters and in particular to *Giovanni Bellini and Giorgione*. By **Bellini:** *Holy Allegory* and the *Lamentation of Christ*; by **Giorgione:** *Moses before the Pharaoh, Judgement of Solomon* and a *Portrait of an Unknown Man*, called the Gattamelata and formerly attributed to others, with works also by **Carpaccio** and **Cima da Conegliano.**

Room XXII - Dedicated to Flemish and German painters of the sixteenth century. It houses works of **Hans Holbein** (*Portrait of Richard Southwell, Self-portrait*), by **Albrecht Altdorfer** (*Stories of San Floriano*), and by **Gerard David** (*Adoration of the Magi*).

Room XXIII - Dedicated to **Correggio,** one of the most important Emilian painters of the sixteenth century. It houses the artist's most important works, such as the famous *Adoration of the Child, Rest on the Flight to Egypt* and the *Madonna in Glory*; in the same room are two portraits attributed to **Raphael** and paintings by **Joos Van Cleve, Giampietrino** and **Bernardino Luini.**

Room XXIV - Also known as the *Gabinetto delle Miniature* (Miniatures Room), it houses a rich collection of Italian and foreign fifteenth and sixteenth-century miniatures.

Second Gallery of the Loggia (E) - The decoration and the frescoes on the ceiling date back to the second half of the seventeenth century. Classical sculptures area also exhibited here including the circular altar depicting the *Sacrifice of Iphigenia*, I century BC Greek art; the *Spinario*, a Roman copy of the Greek original Greek, and the *Seated Girl preparing to dance*, a Roman copy of the Hellenistic original.

Third Gallery of the Loggia (F) - The vaults have been frescoed by various late seventeenth-century painters and the series of ancient statues lining the corridor continues.

Room XXV - Dedicated to **Michelangelo Buonarroti** (1475-1564), it houses the famous Holy Family Roundel, the only one existing painted by the artist in 1505 for the marriage of Agnolo Doni and Maddalena Strozzi; the room also contains works by **Frá Bartolomeo, Albertinelli, Berruguete** and **Rosso Fiorentino.**

Room XXVI - Dedicated to **Raffaello Sanzio** (1483-1520) and **Andrea del Sarto**. By the great master of Urbino: portrait of *Francesco Maria della Rovere, Madonna of the Goldfinch* (1506), portrait of *Julius II* and portrait of *Leo X* (1519). By **Andrea del Sarto**, *Madonna of the Harpies* (1517), his masterpiece, and *The Four Saints*.

Room XXVII - Dedicated to Tuscan mannerists. By **Pontormo**, perhaps the most genial personality of Tuscan mannerism, one can admire *Supper at Emmaus*, one of the artist's finest works, the *Holy Trinity* and others; By Rosso Fiorentino, *Madonna with Child and Saints*.

Room XXVIII - Dedicated to **Titian** (1490-1576), a great figure of sixteenth century Venetian painting who, basing his work on the teachings of Bellini and Giorgione, emphasises chromatic values, thus resolving formal composition problems through the relationship between colour and tone. In this room some of his

Michelangelo: The Holy Family (Tondo Doni).

Rosso Fiorentino: Musician Angel.

34

Raffaello: Our Lady of the Goldfinch.

most famous works are exhibited: The *Venus of Urbino, Venus and Cupid, La Flora*, besides paintings by his pupil, **Palma the Elder** (*Judith*).

Room XXIX - Dedicated to **Parmigianino,** by whom one can admire the *Madonna with the Long Neck* (1534-40) and *Portrait of a Man.*

Room XXX - Also known as the ***Emilian Painters Room***, it contains works of small dimensions by Emilian Masters of the sixteenth century and completes the preceding room.

Room XXXI - Dedicated to **Dosso Dossi**, a painter of Ferrarese origins, but essentially of Venetian culture. In this room, besides works by Dosso, are two notable portraits: The *Fornarina* by **Sebastiano del Piombo** and *Portrait of a Young Man,* by **Lorenzo Lotto.**

Tiziano: Venus of Urbino.

Caravaggio: Adolescent Bacchus.

Canaletto: View of the Dural Palace of Venice.

Room XXXII - Dedicated to **Sebastiano del Piombo** and to sixteenth-century Venetian paintings. One can admire: *Death of Adonis* by Sebastiano del Piombo, *Holy Conversation* by **Lorenzo Lotto** and two portraits of men by **Paris Bordon.**

Room XXXIII - Also known as the *Sixteenth-century Corridor,* it is dedicated to second generation Tuscan and Foreign mannerists, including **Vasari, Bronzino, Allori, Zucchi, Morales** and **Clouet.**

Room XXXIV - Dedicated to **Veronese** (1528-88), the great Venetian artist who depicted the opulent Venetian society of his times with monumental compositions of wide perspective immersed in vibrant and luminous colours. Of his works one can admire, the *Holy Family with St Barbara* and the *Annunciation.*

Room XXXV - Dedicated to **Tintoretto** (1518-1594), a painter who, together with Veronese, dominated the second half of the Venetian sixteenth century. Amongst his works: *Portrait of Sansovino, Leda, Portrait of an Admiral;* in the same room: *Portrait of Francesco Maria II della Rovere* and the *Madonna of the People* by **Barocci.**

Room XXXV-XL - The *Staircase Vestibule* by **Buontalenti** houses: *Marble Boar,* a Roman copy of the Hellenistic original, copied by Pietro Tacca for his famous "Porcellino" in the straw market; *Torso of a Satyr,* from the Pergamene School (II century B.C.). On the walls, seventeenth-century paintings including the *Madonna of the Snow* by **Guido Reni.**

Room XLI - Dedicated to **Rubens** (1577-1640) and seventeenth-century Flemish painting. By Rubens, a painter who gives a passionate view of life in compositions full of warmth and bright colours, the works exhibited are: *Self-portrait, Portrait of Isabella Brandt,* the *Triumphal Entry of Henry IV into Paris* and the *Triumphal Entry of Ferdinand of Austria into Antwerp.* By **Antonio Van Dyck,** a great Flemish portrait painter and a follower of Rubens: *Portrait of Giovanni de Montfort;* by **Giusto Sustermans,** a Flemish painter, for many years the official portrait painter at the court of the Medicis: *Portrait of Galileo.* Of great interest is also the *Self-portrait* of **Diego Velázquez.**

Room XLII - Known as **Room of Niobe,** on account of other statues of Niobe and her children exhibited here. These are Roman copies of Hellenistic originals of the III-II century BC. In the same room, the *Medici Vase* (I century AD).

Room XLIII - This room contains works by Mattia Preti, Bernardo Strozzi and Guercino.

Room XLIV - Dedicated to **Rembrandt** (1606-1669). By the great Dutch painter: the famous *Portrait of an Old Man, Self-portrait of his youth* and *Self-portrait of his old age.* Also in this room, representing Northern genre painting: *The Lunch* by **Jan Steen,** *Landscapes* by **Jacob Ruysdael** and *Landscape with ford* by **Brueghel the Elder.**

Room XLV - Dedicated to Italian and European eighteenth-century paintings. It houses works of the most representative painters of the century's various styles and tastes: *Susanna and the Old Men* by **Giovan Battista Piazzetta;** *Erection* of *the Statue of an Emperor* and *Capricci* by **Francesco Guardi,** *View of the Grand Canal* and *View of the Ducal Palace* by **Canaletto**; *The painter's family* by **Giuseppe Maria Crespi**; *The Confession* by **Pietro Longhi;** *Maria Adelaide in Turkish Dress* by **Jean Etienne Liotard,** *Children Playing* by **Jean Baptiste Chardin** and two paintings depicting *Maria Teresa of Bourbón y Vallabriga Countess of Chinchó* by **Francisco Goya.** Returning to the corridor, one comes to the *Laocoon* group, a copy by **Baccio Bandinelli** (XVI century) of the Hellenistic original in the Vatican; this leads to the terrace of the *Loggia della Signoria* (H), which looks on to the square below. Coming down the Great Staircase by Buontalenti, in the exit hall on the ground floor on can see the *Pomona* statue, a modern work by **Marino Marini.**
On the floor below, five halls were recently opened with works by Caravaggio (Bacchus, The Sacrifice of Isaac and The Medusa) and several of his followers, such as Artemisia Gentileschi (Judith and Holofernes).

6 **ORSANMICHELE CHURCH -** A singular example of fourteenth-century civil and religious architecture, it was built by **Francesco Talenti**, **Neri di Fioravanti** and **Benci di Cione** in 1337 as a corn market-loggia. The church of *San Michele in Orto* (from which the present building takes its name) was built on this site in 895 and replaced in 1290 by the grain store loggia built by **Arnolfo di Cambio.**
When, in 1304, fire destroyed Arnolfo's loggia the present building was constructed; this is a precious example of the change from Gothic to Romanesque style that was taking place at that time. In 1380 this building was used as a place of worship and **Simone Talenti** added to it the majestic palace for use as a granary, closing the external arches with very fine Gothic ornamentation.
On the outside, in the pilasters between the arches, are the *Tabernacles,* above them the emblems of the Major Craft Guilds, containing statues of their patron saints. These sculptures are the work of the most celebrated fourteenth and fifteenth-century sculptors: **Ghiberti** (*St Matthew, St Stephen* and *St John the Baptist*), **Nanni di Banco** (*Four Crowned Saints*), **Donatello** (*St George,* the

original of which is in the Bargello, *St Peter* and *St Mark*), **Verrocchio** (*The doubting of St Thomas*), and **Giambologna** (*St Luke*). The rectangular-shaped *interior* is divided into two naves by pilasters supporting Roman arches and cross vaults. The *frescoes on the pilasters* representing the patron saints of the Minor Guilds are the work of **Giovanni del Ponte, Smeraldo** and **Ambrogio di Baldese.** In the right nave is a splendid *marble Tabernacle,* decorated at the base with small plaques in relief depicting the *Virtues* and *Scenes from the Life of the Virgin;* at the back is an enormous panel in alto-rilievo depicting the *Death and the Assumption of the Virgin* by **Andrea Orcagna** (1349-1359). The panel on the altar, depicting the *Madonna of the Graces* surrounded by Angels, is the work of **Bernardo Daddi** (1347).

Opposite the Church of Orsanmichele is the *Church of St Charles of the Lombards,* begun in 1349 and terminated in 1404. Inside are the *Deposition* by **Niccolò di Pietro Gerini** and the *Glory of St Charles Borromeo* by **Matteo Rosselli.**

GUILDHALL OF THE WOOL MERCHANTS - The Wool Merchants' Guildhall is a picturesque building erected in 1308 **7**

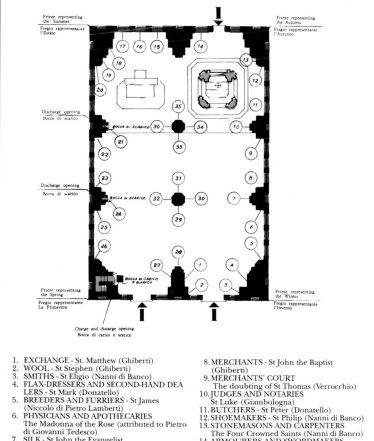

1. EXCHANGE - St. Matthew (Ghiberti)
2. WOOL - St Stephen (Ghiberti)
3. SMITHS - St Eligio (Nanni di Banco)
4. FLAX-DRESSERS AND SECOND-HAND DEALERS - St Mark (Donatello)
5. BREEDERS AND FURRIERS - St James (Niccolò di Pietro Lamberti)
6. PHYSICIANS AND APOTHECARIES
   The Madonna of the Rose (attributed to Pietro di Giovanni Tedesco)
7. SILK - St John the Evangelist (Baccio da Montelupo)
8. MERCHANTS - St John the Baptist (Ghiberti)
9. MERCHANTS' COURT
   The doubting of St Thomas (Verrocchio)
10. JUDGES AND NOTARIES
    St Luke (Giambologna)
11. BUTCHERS - St Peter (Donatello)
12. SHOEMAKERS - St Philip (Nanni di Banco)
13. STONEMASONS AND CARPENTERS
    The Four Crowned Saints (Nanni di Banco)
14. ARMOURERS AND SWORDMAKERS
    St George (Donatello)

Church of Orsanmichele: Tabernacle of Orcagna.

made up of a high tower-house and another lower building which leads to the huge fourteenth-century halls of Orsanmichele by means of a footbridge.

It was the headquarters of one of the most prosperous and powerful Guilds: the *Wool-Merchants' Guild*, which in the twelfth century numbered over 30,000 craftsmen and bore the *Agnus Dei* on its coat-of-arms. Restored at the beginning of the twentieth century, it is now the headquarters of the Società Dantesca (Dante Society).

On the side of the building that looks out on to Via Orsanmichele is the *Gothic Tabernacle* of *Santa Maria della Tromba*. In this Tabernacle, once in Piazza del Mercato Vecchio, a panel depicting the *Madonna Enthroned* and the *Coronation,* by **Jacopo del Casentino**, is preserved.

8 **PIAZZA DEL DUOMO** - Together with *Piazza San Giovanni,* it makes up the religious centre of the city where the *Baptistery,* the *Bell Tower* and the *Duomo* stand: the three monumental buildings were erected at different times but harmonise perfectly, thanks to the polychromy and to the characteristic geometric marble covering. In the same square, opposite the Bell Tower, is the *Loggia del Bigallo.*

9 **LOGGIA DEL BIGALLO** - A late Gothic building by **Arnoldo Arnoldi**, it was the seat of the first Misericordia Brotherhood founded in the thirteenth century. Inside the loggia a small *Museum* has recently been opened to house the works commissioned by the Bigallo Captains from the fourteenth to the eighteenth century.

Among these works, of significant documentary and artistic value is a fresco dating back to the middle of the fourteenth century of the *Madonna della Misericordia*, with the oldest view of the city, showing the façade and the Duomo Bell Tower during its construction and the church of Santa Reparata which was later demolished.

BAPTISTERY - Dante called this Baptistery il "bel San Giovanni". It is one of the most beautiful examples of Romanesque architecture in Tuscany. Built in the eleventh century, probably on the site of a small paleochristian church dedicated to St Saviour, it has an octagonal plan with a pyramid roof. The facing of green marble from Prato and white marble from Carrara in geometric design (thirteenth century) harmonises the exterior with the volumetric architecture of its interior. **10**

Of great interest are the ***three bronze doors***; the first (1330), on the south side, is by **Andrea Pisano**, a work which marks the beginning of Florentine Gothic sculpture; the second (1403-24), on the northern side, is again Gothic, by **Ghiberti,** who was preferred to Brunelleschi who had presented a project that was already in Renaissance style at a competition held in 1401; the third (1425-52), on the eastern side, is again the work of **Ghiberti** who had by then learned something of Renaissance style and applied the rules of perspective for the first time.

The first door illustrates *Stories from the life of John the Baptist* and the *Cardinal and Theological Virtues*; the second illustrates *Stories from the New Testament*, the *Gospels* and *Doctors of the Church*; the third, admired also by Michelangelo, who said that it was "the door of Paradise", is a series of ten panels depicting *Stories from the Old*

Baptistery, Cathedral and Giotto's Bell Tower.

Testament. The originals are preserved in the Cathedral Museum. The ***Interior,*** austere and classic, repeats the marble decorations of the exterior; the apse, known as the "Scarsella", was added in the thirteenth century. The vault is lined with magnificent mosaics in Byzantine style depicting the *Celestial Hierarchies,* in the second and third bands *Stories from Genesis, Stories of Mary and Jesus, Stories of John the Baptist* and the *Last Judgement,* all works of Florentine and Venetian masters of the thirteenth century. Of special interest are: the marble baptismal font with reliefs by the Pisan school (1371), and the *Sepulchre of Giovanni XXIII, the Antipope,* two works by **Donatello** and **Michelozzo** (1427).

The door known as Ghiberti's 'Paradise'.

42

Baptistry: Interior of the cupola decorated with mosaics (13th cent.).

CATHEDRAL - It was begun by **Arnolfo di Cambio** in 1296 on the **11**
site of the ancient Cathedral of Santa Reparata (the foundations
have been brought to light during recent excavations). The
construction of the building proceeded slowly, first under the
direction of **Giotto** from 1334 to 1336, then under **Francesco
Talenti** and **Lapo Ghini**. Between interruptions, the central nave
was built in 1378, the aisles in 1380, the tribune and the tambour of
the dome between 1380 and 1421.
The *Dome of Brunelleschi,* whose plans were approved after a few
disagreements (1418), was completed in 1434. In 1436 Pope
Eugene IV consecrated the church, dedicating it to Santa Maria del
Fiore.
Several styles have been adopted for this monumental work,
Romanesque and Gothic elements are mixed together, whilst the
superb octagonal dome is an expression of Renaissance rationality.
The façade designed by Arnolfo in Romanesque style and re-
elaborated in Gothic style by Talenti, was completed in 1887 by
Emilio de Fabris.
The *interior,* severe and majestic, is in the shape of a Latin cross
divided into three ample naves by huge composite pilasters topped
by arches and ogival vaults which give impetus to the entire
building. The magnificent polychrome marble floor is attributed to
Baccio d'Agnolo.

Internal façade - The three round *glass windows* are from cartoons
by **Ghiberti** (1413); the *clock* with the four Heads of Prophets in the
corners, is the work of **Paolo Uccello** (1443); the *tomb* of Bishop
Antonio d'Orso is by **Tino da Camaino** (1312).

Right nave - the glass windows are fourteenth century; the bust of
Brunelleschi, whose tomb was found in the crypt of Santa Reparata
in 1972, is by **Buggiano** (1446); the bust of Giotto is by **Benedetto da
Maiano** (1490); the bust of the humanist Marsilio Ficino is by
Andrea Ferrucci (1521).

43

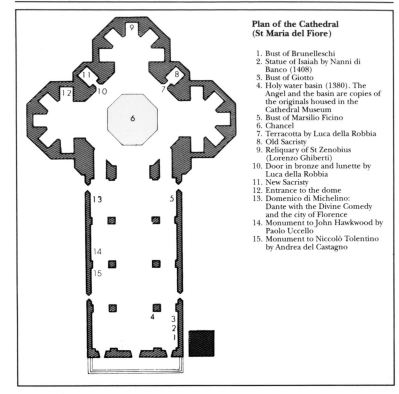

**Plan of the Cathedral
(St Maria del Fiore)**

1. Bust of Brunelleschi
2. Statue of Isaiah by Nanni di Banco (1408)
3. Bust of Giotto
4. Holy water basin (1380). The Angel and the basin are copies of the originals housed in the Cathedral Museum
5. Bust of Marsilio Ficino
6. Chancel
7. Terracotta by Luca della Robbia
8. Old Sacristy
9. Reliquary of St Zenobius (Lorenzo Ghiberti)
10. Door in bronze and lunette by Luca della Robbia
11. New Sacristy
12. Entrance to the dome
13. Domenico di Michelino: Dante with the Divine Comedy and the city of Florence
14. Monument to John Hawkwood by Paolo Uccello
15. Monument to Niccolò Tolentino by Andrea del Castagno

Aerial view of the religious centre.

44

Cathedral: Interior.

Tribune and Apse - The immense octagonal drum is dominated by the *cupola*, a technical and artistic masterpiece by **Filippo Brunelleschi**; the frescoes are by **Vasari** and his assistants (1572-79) with scenes from the *Last Judgement*. The windows are from cartoons by famous artists of the early Renaissance period: **Ghiberti** (*Presentation at the Temple, Prayer in the Garden, Ascension*); **Paolo Uccello** (*Resurrection, Nativity*); **Donatello** (*Crowning of the Virgin*); **Andrea del Castagno** (*Deposition*). The lunettes of the portals of the *Old Sacristy* and the *New Sacristy*, at the corners between the central tribune and the two lateral ones, depict respectively the *Ascension* and the *Resurrection*, in glazed terracotta by **Luca della Robbia.** The bronze door of the New Sacristy was realised by the same artist together with **Michelozzo** and **Maso di Bartolomeo** (1469).
The marble choir gallery, in relief, and the High Altar are the works of **Baccio Bandinelli** and **Giovanni Bandini** (1555), whilst the wooden *Crucifix a*bove the altar is by **Benedetto da Maiano** (1497).

Left Nave - The stained glass windows are fourteenth century: a panel by **Domenico di Michelino** (1465) depicts *Dante and the Divine Comedy* with in the background, on the right, a glimpse of mid-fifteenth century Florence, in the centre Purgatory, on the left Hell and above Paradise. In the third bay a fresco in chiaroscuro depicts the English condottiere, *John Hawkwood* on horseback, who served the Florentine Republic; this is an important work by **Paolo Uccello** (1436). In the second bay is another fresco by **Andrea del Castagno**, also in chairoscuro (1456), and shows the equestrian statue of *Niccolò da Tolentino* (Niccolò Maruzzi); in the first bay is a bust of Arnolfo di Cambio by Ulisse Cambi (1843) and another of Emilio de Fabris (the architect of the façade) by Vincenzo Consani (1887).

Paolo Uccello: Giovanni Acuto.   *A. del Castagno: Niccolò da Tolentino.*

Cupola of Brunelleschi: The last Judgement, detail.

Crypt of Santa Reparata - A staircase between the first and second pilasters of the right nave leads down to the crypt. Excavations began in 1966, lasted almost four years and led to the discovery of the ancient *Church of Santa Reparata,* destroyed in 1375 in order to build the present cathedral.

The excavations brought to light what remained of the original fourth and fifth century church, which had a basilica plan (an apse and three naves): fragments of mosaic flooring, fourteenth-century frescoes, inscriptions, grave-stones and coats-of- arms.

Domenico di Michelino: Dante and his Poem, detail.

Climb to the Dome - The small doors at the end of the two side naves give on to a narrow staircase, with 463 steps, that leads to the dome; one first reaches the internal gallery and then the external one (91 m) which surrounds the lantern (107 m); from here one can enjoy a splendid view of the city and surrounding hills. This visit is recommended in order to appreciate the structure of the dome with its double spherical vault.

GIOTTO'S BELL TOWER - With its square plan and height of 84.70 m, it is a magnificent example of Florentine Gothic style. It **12**

Cathedral of Santa Reparata: Tomb Stones.

Brunelleschi's Dome.

was designed by **Giotto**, who began it in 1334 and directed the works up to the first cornice. On his death **Andrea Pisano**, leaving aside the original project, added another floor, arriving up to the second cornice. Between 1348 and 1359 **Francesco Talenti** built the upper floors with the beautiful two and three mullioned windows scrupulously following Giotto's design, with the exception of the spire which he substituted with jutting horizontal crowning. The harmony and elegance of the architecture's plastic forms are emphasised by the geometric polychrome marble facing which makes the tower appear so slender and graceful. The base is decorated by valuable sculptures and by two bas-reliefs with hexagonal plaques depicting: *Stories from Genesis*, the *History of Human Labour*, the *Planets*, the *Virtues*, the *Liberal Arts* and the *Sacraments*, all by eminent sculptors of that time: **Andrea Pisano, Luca della Robbia, Arnoldo Arnoldi** and **Donatello.** Today the originals, which have been replaced here by copies, are in the Cathedral Museum.

The upper band with four niches on each side contains copies of the statues of *Prophets, Sybils* and *John the Baptist*, also currently housed in the Cathedral Museum.

CATHEDRAL MUSEUM - (9, Piazza del Duomo) Founded in 1891, **13** it houses sculptures, gold work, embroidery, models and designs which were found in the Baptistery, the Duomo and Bell Tower.
At the centre of the stairs leading to the upper floor is the famous *Pietà* by **Michelangelo** (1550-53), an unfinished and dramatic work, sculpted by the artist for his own memorial chapel which he wished to be built in the church of Santa Maria Maggiore in Rome.

Giotto's Bell Tower.

The remains of the old *baptismal font* come from the Baptistery; the antique *silver altar,* masterpiece of Florentine goldsmithery of the fourteenth and fifteenth centuries, made up of 27 plaques, 12 of which depict Stories of St John the Baptist; the wooden statue of the *Repentant Mary Magdalen* is a dramatic work of **Donatello**'s full maturity.

The *statues* are from the Duomo and were used to decorate the façade. They are works of such artists as: **Arnolfo di Cambio, Donatello, Nanni di Banco;** the two famous *choir galleries,* at one time above the entrance doors to the Sacristy, are masterpieces of Renaissance sculpture: the one depicting the last Psalm of David is by **Luca della Robbia** (1431-38), and the other, with a lively dance of singing putti, is by **Donatello** (1433-38), who also created *Moses* and *Jeremiah* and *Habakkuk.*

The complete series of sculptured decorations comes from the Bell-Tower. Of particular interest are the *plaques* sculpted by **Andrea Pisano** to a design allegedly by Giotto.

The Museum also preserves priceless paintings, reliquaries, holy robes, a well-known sixteenth-century drawing of a reconstruction of the Duomo's original façade, a *wooden model of the dome lantern* and in two rooms, especially set up on the ground floor, the tools used by Brunelleschi to build the dome.

Michelangelo's "Pietà".

Opera del Duomo: Choir by Donatello.

Donatello: Magdalene, the prophets Abacuc and Jeremiah.

51

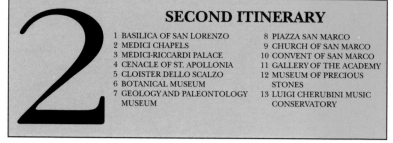

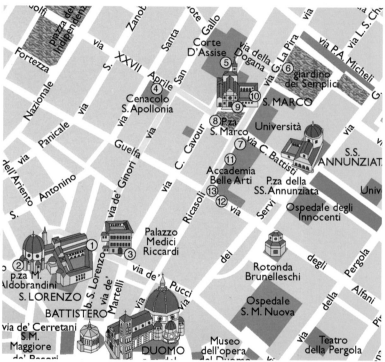

1 **BASILICA OF SAN LORENZO** (Piazza S. Lorenzo) A masterpiece of religious architecture of the early Renaissance period, it was rebuilt by **Brunelleschi** on the site of a pre-existing church (393), consecrated by St Ambrose, commissioned by Cosimo I the Elder in 1419, and finished, following the original project, in 1460 by **Antonio Manetti.**

The *interior* is shaped like a Latin cross with a nave and side aisles divided by columns and has a coffered ceiling. At the end of the nave stand two bronze *pulpits* which are the last works of **Donatello** (1460). The *internal façade* is by **Michelangelo.** In the right nave, on the second altar is *Marriage of Mary* by **Rosso Fiorentino;** at the back is a beautiful marble *shrine* by **Desiderio da Settignano.** On the High Altar is the *Crucifix* by **Baccio da Montelupo** and under the altar three circular bronze gratings show the tomb of Cosimo the Elder in the crypt below.

At the back of the left arm of the transept is the *Old Sacristy* (1420-29) by **Brunelleschi** designed as a square surmounted by a small hemispherical dome, which with its perfect geometric shape

52

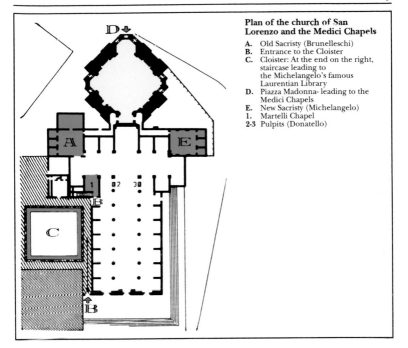

Plan of the church of San Lorenzo and the Medici Chapels

A. Old Sacristy (Brunelleschi)
B. Entrance to the Cloister
C. Cloister: At the end on the right, staircase leading to the Michelangelo's famous Laurentian Library
D. Piazza Madonna- leading to the Medici Chapels
E. New Sacristy (Michelangelo)
1. Martelli Chapel
2-3 Pulpits (Donatello)

The Basilica of S. Lorenzo.

expresses the Renaissance concept of space. The sculptured decorations by **Donatello**, four medallions in polychrome plaster with *Stories of St. John the Evangelist*, four polychrome terracotta roundels with the *Evangelists*, two *bronze shutters* and the architecture of the doors make this refined setting even more precious. Also to be found here is the sarcophagus of Piero and Giovanni de' Medici in porphyry and bronze, a work by **Verrocchio**. Still in the left transept, in the Martelli chapel, are the sepulchral monument by **Donatello** and the *Annunciation* by **Filippo Lippi**. From the church, through the splendid *fifteenth-century cloister* in Brunelleschi style, one reaches the *Laurentian Library*, instituted by Cosimo the Elder,

53

Basilica of St. Lorenzo: Interior.

enlarged and enriched by Lorenzo from whom it took its name. It is the work of **Michelangelo's** architectural genius (1524), also responsible for the *Vestibule* and for furnishing the library which houses a rich collection of illuminated manuscripts.

2 **THE MEDICI CHAPELS** (6, piazza Madonna degli Aldobrandini). From the huge *crypt* designed by **Buontalenti**, where many members of the Medici family are buried, a short staircase leads to the monumental *Chapel of the Princes* in baroque style, begun by **Nigetti** in 1604 from Giovanni de' Medici's design. It is octagonal and the walls are entirely covered with semi-precious stones. It is crowned by a large dome with *Stories from Genesis* and the *Last Judgement* frescoed by **Pietro Benvenuti** in 1828. Standing against the walls are *six large mausoleums* dedicated to the Grand Dukes, two of which are surmounted by gilded bronze statues of **Pietro** and **Fernando Tacca**. At the base are the coats-of-arms of sixteen Tuscan cities that were part of the Grand Duchy.

From this Chapel, passing through a corridor, one arrives at the

Interior of the chapel of the Princes.

54

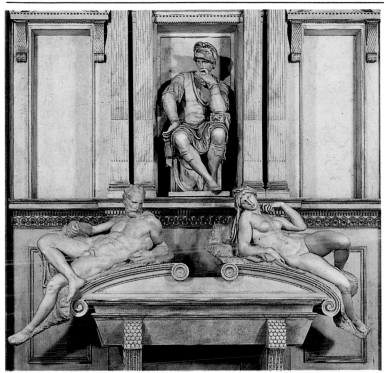

Michelangelo: Monument to Lorenzo De' Medici, detail.

Michelangelo: Triple staircase of the vestibule.

New Sacristy by **Michelangelo**, a true square sepulchral chapel surmounted by a lacunar dome. It was so called to distinguish it from the Old Sacristy by Brunelleschi, commissioned by Leo X and Clement VII to house the tombs of Lorenzo the Magnificent and Giuliano de' Medici (murdered during the Pazzi conspiracy) and other members of the family.

Begun in 1520 by Michelangelo who worked on it intermittently

55

until 1537 and continued by Vasari, it was however never finished. Entering on the left: the **Tomb of Lorenzo**, Duke of Urbino with the allegorical statues of *Dawn* and *Dusk*, in front of it is the **Tomb of Giuliano**, Duke of Nemours, with the figures of *Day* and *Night*. The Dukes, Giuliano and Lorenzo are in a dominating position over the sarcophagi where the figures of Time lie in the manner of scrolls. On the entrance wall, to the right, is the unfinished *Tomb* of *Lorenzo the Magnificent* and his brother Giuliano, with the *Madonna and Child* at the top and at the sides the statues of two saints, *Cosima and Damiano* by the pupils Giovanni da Montorsoli and Raffaello da Montelupo.

The whole, designed as a harmonic synthesis of architecture and sculpture (only here in fact could Michelangelo achieve a perfect blend between the statues and their surroundings), is probably intended to denote the fate of the soul after death: a destiny of resurrection, which here takes the Christian shape of the Madonna and Child, contemplated by the two Dukes, representing Action (Giuliano) and Thought (Lorenzo), and of deliverance from the ravages of Time, symbolised here by the four allegorical figures.

Mural Drawings by Michelangelo and his School: From the door opposite the entrance one arrives (by request) at the room under the apse of the Chapel, on whose walls 56 drawings of human figures of remarkable dimensions have recently been discovered and restored, almost all of which are attributed to **Michelangelo** - a kind of "mural note" by the artist. Other architectural drawings and sketches, half of which attributed to the great Master and half to his pupils, can be seen in the apse of the New Sacristy.

3 **MEDICI-RICCARDI PALACE** (1, via Cavour) - Magnificent example of a Florentine Renaissance palace, built by **Michelozzo,** (1444-64) for Cosimo the Elder. It was the residence of the Medici family from Lorenzo the Magnificent to Cosimo I; subsequently enlarged, it was bought by the Riccardi family in 1655. The *façade* in which the idea of upwardly declining rustication is introduced, is scanned by centrally mullioned windows and crowned by a superb, sharply over-hanging cornice. The porticoed internal square

Michelozzo: The Medici-Riccardi Palace.

Benozzo Gozzoli: The journey of the Magi - Lorenzo il Magnifico, detail.

together with the loggia above, forms a typical fifteenth-century Florentine palace courtyard. In the *Chapel*, also by Michelozzo, one can admire the beautiful *Procession of the Magi*, a fresco by **Benozzo Gozzoli** (1459-60).

On the altar is a contemporary copy of the *Nativity* by **Filippo Lippi**, which is now in Berlin. The Palace is now used partly as a library (it houses in fact the *Biblioteca Riccardiana e Moreniana*), partly as the *Medici Museum,* where tapestries, portraits and paintings (including paintings by Lippi, Bronzino and Ghirlandaio) are preserved, and partly as public offices.

The *Gallery* is used as a conference room; the frescoes are by **Luca Giordano,** whose services the Riccardi family managed to obtain, in spite of the Medicis.

THE CENACLE OF ST. APOLLONIA (1, via XXVII Aprile) - An ancient monastery of the Camaldolensian order, it dates back to the eleventh century, and was restored during the fourteenth and fifteenth centuries; recent restoration work brought to light the *Renaissance Cloister.*
In the *Refectory* **Andrea del Castagno** painted in 1450 the *Last Supper,* a realistic and dramatic work, considered to be one of the fundamental stages of Florentine Renaissance painting; besides this work, it is worth recalling the *Crucifixion,* the *Deposition* and the *Resurrection,* the sinopias of which are also on display.

4

5 CLOISTER DELLO SCALZO (69, via Cavour) - Known also as the cloister of St John the Baptist, it belonged to the brotherhood of the Scalzi (Bare-footed) monks. A small sixteenth-century cloister, it was frescoed in chiaroscuro with *Scenes from the Life of St John the Baptist* by **Andrea del Sarto** (1526). After being removed and restored, the frescoes have now been replaced in loco.

6 BOTANICAL MUSEUM (4, via La Pira) - One of the most important in Italy on account of its extensive collection of herbariums and plants, it adjoins the *Botanical Gardens* (entrance from 3, via Micheli), which the old *Semplici Garden*, founded by Cosimo I in 1545 which still today boasts a precious collection of exotic plants.

7 GEOLOGY AND PALEONTOLOGY MUSEUM (4, Via La Pira) - This museum was founded by Grand Duke Cosimo I and constantly enriched by his Medici and Lorraine successors.
In addition to a great number of fossils from various Italian regions, those found during excavations in the Upper Valdarno are of particular interest.

8 PIAZZA SAN MARCO - The square is surrounded on the west side by the eighteenth-century *Palazzina della Livia* and on the east side by the lovely fourteenth-century *Loggia* of the ancient Hospital of St Matthew, seat of the Academy of Fine Arts and Florence University, and to the North by the *Church and Convent of St Mark*. The monument to Manfredo Fanti (1873) in the centre of the square is by **Pio Fedi**.

9 CHURCH OF SAN MARCO - Built by **Michelozzo** in 1452 on the site of the church of the Silvestrini monks, it underwent frequent modification during the following centuries. The *interior,* with a single nave and carved ceiling, houses valuable works of the school of Giotto, including works by Frá Bartolomeo and Gherardini. Of particular interest is the *Sacristy* by Michelozzo, the Serragli Chapel and the St Antonino Chapel by **Giambologna**. The façade which dates back to 1780, is by Gioacchino Pronti.

Facade of St. Mark Church.

CONVENT OF SAN MARCO - Ancient convent of the Silvestrini monks, rebuilt by **Michelozzo** (1452-62), by commission of Cosimo the Elder, it was one of the principal spiritual and artistic centres of Renaissance Florence. Beato Angelico lived and worked here, as did St Antonino, Savonarola and Frà Bartolomeo. The convent passed to the Government in 1860 and after 1920 was transformed into a *Museum.* From the Renaissance cloister *Chiostro di Sant'Antonino* one enters the ancient *Pilgrims' Hospice Room*, where there are panels painted by **Frà Angelico** for Florentine and Tuscan churches, including the *Last Judgement*, the *Flax-dressers' Tabernacle*, the *Deposition* of Santa Trinita, the *Altar-piece* of St. Mark and the *Lamentation,* which comes from the Compagnia del Tempio; In the "Lavabo" Room and the old *Refectory of the Silvestrini Monks* are conserved the works of **Frà Bartolomeo**; The *Chapter Room* is dominated by the *Crucifixion* by **Angelico**. At the foot of the stairs leading to the first floor there is a small *Refectory* where **Domenico del Ghirlandaio** frescoed the *Last Supper* in circa 1433. At the top of the stairs in the corridor on the first floor, one can admire the beautiful *Annunciation* and *Crucifixion* by **Angelico**. The *Cells* are decorated by **Angelico** and his pupils following a precise meditation programme for the friars. At the end of the corridor are the *Prior's apartments* where Savonarola lodged, while to the right of the entrance is the *Library,* designed by **Michelozzo,** a work of purity and stylistic rigour, typical of the Renaissance period.

10

GALLERY OF THE ACADEMY (60, via Ricasoli) - It was founded in 1784, when the Grand Duke Pietro Leopoldo wanted to gather

11

Ghirlandaio: The Last Supper, detail.

Beato Angelico: The "Universal Judgment", detail of the Elected.

Beato Angelico: Annunciation.

together in a single academy the different schools of drawing that existed in Florence, adding a collection of paintings by old masters. It houses in fact a rich collection of works of the Florentine school, right from its origins to the sixteenth century; from 1873 it has been enriched with an exceptional collection of *Michelangelo's sculptures*. These sculptures are arranged along the walls of the big hall to which the **Tribune of David** forms the backdrop, dominated by the very famous statue sculpted between 1501 and 1504, commissioned by the Opera del Duomo and which the Florentines wanted to place in Piazza della Signoria as a symbol of the Republic's freedom. The colossal statue (4.23 metres high) the culminating work of the artist's youth, was made from a single block of marble found by **Michelangelo** in the courtyard of the Cathedral Museum; it had been abandoned there by Agostino di Duccio. Even though it recalls the classical style of Belvedere's Apollo, the statue, greatly admired by his contemporaries, with its expressive intensity

David of Michelangelo.

Gallery of the Academy: Cassone Adimari, detail.

and the evident anatomical research undertaken by the artist, combines all the characteristics of Michelangelo's work and expresses the concept that Buonarroti, and indeed the entire Renaissance, had of Man.

In this vast room other masterpieces by the great master can be admired: the *Pietà*, known as the *Palestrina*, a late work in which the contrast between the dressed shapes of the inert Christ and the unfinished figures holding up his body, emphasise the tragicalness of the subject; the four rough cast *Prisoners* designed for the tomb of Julius II, where the unfinished carving expresses with powerful dramatic force and plastic vigour, Michelangelo's concept of the liberation of form from matter, of the spirit from the body; *St Matthew*, the only one of the series of twelve Apostles intended for the Cathedral façade, although unfinished, documents the creative ideas of Michelangelo. The *bronze bust* of Michelangelo is the work of his friend and pupil **Daniele da Volterra.**

The Academy also houses two interesting plaster models by **Giambologna.** The *Rape of the Sabine Women* (the original is under the Loggia della Signoria) and *Virtue overcoming Vice* (the original is in the Bargello).

12 **MUSEUM OF PRECIOUS STONES** (78, via degli Alfani) - Founded in 1588 by Ferdinand I de' Medici, the Semi-precious Stone workshop obtained success and fame for over two centuries. The *Museum* today houses precious examples of Florentine mosaics.

13 **LUIGI CHERUBINI MUSIC CONSERVATORY** (2, piazzetta delle Belle Arti) - Besides the collection of books and autographed works by well-known Italian composers (Monteverdi-Rossini-Cherubini) housed in the *Music Library,* it is possible to admire in the adjoining *Museum* a rich collection of precious and antique musical instruments.

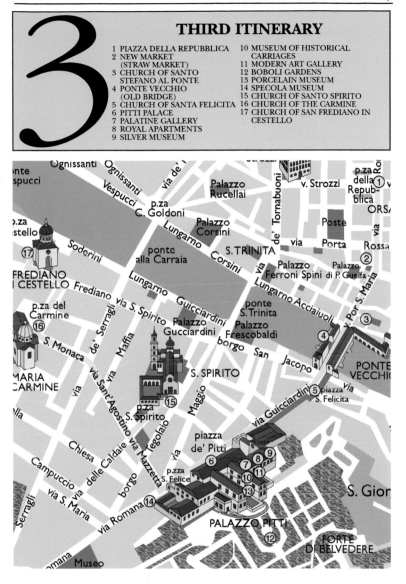

THIRD ITINERARY

1 PIAZZA DELLA REPUBBLICA
2 NEW MARKET
  (STRAW MARKET)
3 CHURCH OF SANTO
  STEFANO AL PONTE
4 PONTE VECCHIO
  (OLD BRIDGE)
5 CHURCH OF SANTA FELICITA
6 PITTI PALACE
7 PALATINE GALLERY
8 ROYAL APARTMENTS
9 SILVER MUSEUM
10 MUSEUM OF HISTORICAL
   CARRIAGES
11 MODERN ART GALLERY
12 BOBOLI GARDENS
13 PORCELAIN MUSEUM
14 SPECOLA MUSEUM
15 CHURCH OF SANTO SPIRITO
16 CHURCH OF THE CARMINE
17 CHURCH OF SAN FREDIANO IN
   CESTELLO

PIAZZA DELLA REPUBBLICA - Between the religious and political **1** centre was the picturesque piazza del Mercato Vecchio, site of the old market place, demolished in 1887, in order to build the present piazza della Repubblica. Flanked by nineteenth-century palaces and closed by arcades at the back, it is now the modern city centre. On the *column* that rises almost in the centre of the square is a copy of the statue of *Abundance* which replaces the original that stood here when it was the site of the Old Market.

NEW MARKET - This is an elegant loggia in Renaissance style built **2** by **Giovanni B. del Tasso** (1551), under which the silk merchants and goldsmiths used to gather. It is also called "del Porcellino" (of the little pig), due to the famous bronze wild boar sculptured by

Neri di Fioravante: Ponte Vecchio.

Pietro Tacca: The "Porcellino".

Pietro Tacca in 1612 (a copy of the antique one in marble preserved in the Uffizi Gallery), which decorates the fountain. In the characteristic New Market or "della Paglia" (Straw) products typical of Florentine craftsmanship are on sale.

3 **CHURCH OF SANTO STEFANO AL PONTE** - The *Church of St Stephen and St Cecily* is in a small square to the left of via Por S. Maria. Tradition has it that the church dates back to the time of Charlemagne. The oldest part of the façade is the lower half (1233) which is enriched by small mullioned windows and a white and green marble facing, typical of the Florentine Romanesque style of that period. The ***interior*** originally had a nave and two aisles. It was extensively restored by **Tacca** (1649-55) who transformed it into a single large nave with an open trussed roof, decorated with sixteenth-century altars, a scenographic *presbytery* by **Buontalenti** (1574), a bronze relief of the *Stoning of St. Stephen* by **Tacca** and paintings by **Jacopo di Cione, Santi di Tito** and **Matteo Rosselli.** The diocese museum of sacred art holds works from diocese churches that can no longer be used for worship or which cannot guarantee their safety.

PONTE VECCHIO - Probably already existing during the Roman period it is the most ancient and characteristic bridge in Florence. Destroyed by the River Arno when it flooded in 1333, it was rebuilt by **Neri di Fioravante** (although according to Vasari, by Taddeo Gaddi) in 1345. It is flanked by shops on either side which Ferdinand I, towards the end of the sixteenth century, granted to the goldsmiths; above the upstream row of shops is the ***Corridoio Vasariano*** (Vasari Corridor) which joins Palazzo Vecchio to the Pitti

4

Neri di Fioravante: Ponte Vecchio.

Palace. On the central terrace, on the right of the bridge is a bronze bust of the Florentine goldsmith, Benvenuto Cellini.

CHURCH OF SANTA FELICITA - (piazza S. Felicità) Built on the site of an ancient Christian cemetery and a paleochristian oratory, it was restored in the eleventh and fourteenth centuries. The front porch, by **Vasari,** was left intact by **Ruggeri** when he completely rebuilt the church in 1736. The ***interior*** consists of a single nave divided by pilaster strips, with chapels between; the first on the right, the *Capponi Chapel,* is by **Brunelleschi.** Above the altar: *Deposition* by **Pontormo;** the fresco of the *Annunciation* on the right is also by **Pontormo.**

5

PITTI PALACE - This is the most monumental of the Renaissance Florentine palaces. It was commissioned by Luca Pitti and built by Luca Fancelli in 1458, probably after a design by **Brunelleschi** (1440). It was extended in later centuries by Ammannati, Parigi and Ruggeri. In 1549 it was bought by Eleonora di Toledo, wife of Cosimo I and became the home of the Grand Dukes. After the death of the last of the Medicis, it passed to the Lorraine family and during the time when Florence was capital, from 1865 to 1871, it

6

GIARDINO

Pitti Palace
Palatine Gallery
First floor

I	Venus Room
II	Apollo Room
III	Mars Room
IV	Jupiter Room
V	Saturn Room
VI	Iliad Room
VII	Room with the Stove
VIII	Jupiter's Education Room
IX	Bathroom
X	Ulysses Room
XI	Prometheus Room
XII	Corridors of Columns
XIII	Justice Room
XIV	Flora Room
XV	Putti Room
XVI	Poccetti Gallery
XVII	Music Room
XVIII	Castagnoli Room
XIX-XXIII	Volterrano Apartments
XXIV-XXVIII	Rooms closed to the public

A. Vestibule
B. Cup Room
C. Terrace
D. Ammannati Courtyard

Royal apartaments

1.2	Vestibule
3	Gallery of statues
4	Dining or Niche Room
5	Green Room
6	Throne Room
7	Blue Room
8	Chapel
9	Parrots Room
10	Yellow Room
11	Queen's Chamber
12	King's Chamber
13	Study
14	Sitting Room
15	Antechamber
16	Bona Room
17	Ballroom (or White Room)

Pitti Palace: Facade.

was the residence of the Royal Family. Now it is the home of important museums: the *Palatine Gallery,* the *Royal Apartments*, the *Silver Museum,* the *Modern Art Gallery*, the *Museum of Historical Carriages,* while the small buildings in the garden house the *Porcelain Museum.*

7 PALATINE GALLERY - One of the most selective art galleries where one can admire the principal masterpieces of exponents of Italian and European schools from the fifteenth to the eighteenth centuries. Begun in 1620 by Cosimo II, the collection was greatly

66

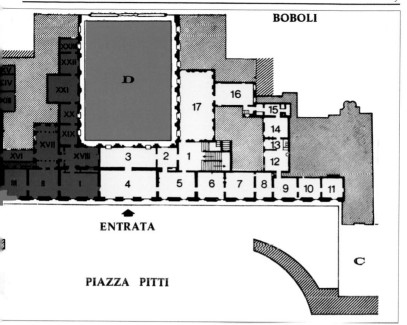

extended by Ferdinand II. In 1820 the Palatine Gallery was opened
to the public by the Lorraine family and in 1911 passed to the
Government. The works are not arranged to the usual pattern but
instead follow the more traditional form of a Prince's private
gallery, an arrangement which, though less rational, remains
nevertheless a precious example of the taste of past collectors. One
enters the Palatine Gallery through the Palace's main *Staircase*, built
by **Ammannati**, through the *Vestibule* (1-2), the *Gallery of Statues* (3)
and the *Niches Room* (4) and on to the **Venus Room** (I); this is
decorated like the other four rooms, by **Piero da Cortona** and **Ciro
Ferri,** with stuccoes and frescoes having as a theme mythological
figures exalting the Medici family. In this room **Titian's** paintings
are exhibited; *The Concert* (probably painted in collaboration with
Giorgione), *Portrait of Jules II, Portrait of Pietro Aretino, Portrait of a
Noble Lady* (known as "*The Beauty*"); by **Rubens**: *Peasants returning
from work, Ulysses in the island of the Phaeacians;* and by **Salvator Rosa**:
Two seascapes at Sunset. In the centre, *Italian Venus* by **Antonio
Canova** (1810).
In the **Apollo Room** (II), there are more works by **Titian**: *Portrait of
a Gentleman* and *Mary Magdalen;* by **Andrea del Sarto**: *Deposition* and
the *Holy Family;* by **Rosso Fiorentino**: *Madonna Enthroned and Saints;*
by **Van Dyck**: *Portrait of Charles of England* and *Henrietta of France.*
In the **Mars Room** (III) works by **Murillo**: *Madonna with Child* and
Madonna with Rosary; by **Rubens**: *The Four Philosophers* and
Consequences of War; by **Van Dyck**: *Portrait of Cardinal Guido
Bentivoglio;* by **Veronese**: *Portrait of a Man;* by **Titian**: *Portrait of
Cardinal Ippolito de' Medici;* by **Guido Reni**: *Cleopatra;* by **Tintoretto**:
Portrait of Luigi Cornaro.
In the **Jupiter Room** (IV) works by **Andrea del Sarto**: *Our Lady of the
Assumption,* the *Annunciation* and *St John the Baptist;* by **Frá
Bartolomeo**: *Deposition* and *St. Mark;* by **Rubens**: *Nymphs and Satyrs*

Rubens: The Consequences of the War.

Raffaello: Our Lady of the Chair.

and the *Holy Family;* by **Bronzino**: *Portrait of Guidobaldo della Rovere,*
by **Borgognone**: *Battle;* by **Raphael**: the *Veiled Lady;* by **Perugino**:
Madonna with Bag; by **Guercino**: *Madonna of the swallow.*
In the **Saturn Room** works by **Raphael**: *Madonna of the Grand Duke,*
Portrait of Tommaso Inghirami, Vision of Ezekiel, Portrait of Agnolo and
Maddalena Doni, Portrait of Cardinal Bernardo Dovizi, and the

Madonna of the Chair; by **Guercino**: *St Peter;* by **Andrea del Sarto**: *Dispute of the Trinity;* by **Perugino:** *Deposition* and *Mary Magdalen;* by **Frà Bartolomeo**: *Jesus Risen from the Dead with the Evangelists.*

In the **Iliad Room** (VI), frescoed by **Luigi Sabatelli** (1819), there are works by **Raphael**: *Portrait of a Pregnant woman;* by **Andrea del Sarto**: two *Assumptions;* by **Ridolfo del Ghirlandaio**: *Portrait of a Woman;* by **Sustermans**: *Portrait of Count Valdemaro Cristiano*; by **Velàzquez**: *Portrait of Philip IV of Spain.* The statue of *Charity* in the centre of the room is by **Lorenzo Bertolini** (1824).

In the **Room with the Stove** (VII), with walls frescoed by **Pietro da Cortona**, **Jupiter's Education Room** (VIII) with *Sleeping Cupid* by **Caravaggio**, and *Judith* by **Allori**, the **Bathroom** (IX) in Empire style; **Room of Ulysses** (X) with the *Madonna of the Window-pane (Impannata)* by **Raphael** (1514), *Mary Magdalen* by **Dolci** and other works by **Tintoretti**, **Andrea del Sarto** and **Guido Reni**; **Prometheus Room** (XI) with the *Holy Family* by **Signorelli**; *Madonna with Child* by **Filippo Lippi** and other works by **Botticelli**, **Pontormo** and **Giulio Romano**; The **Corridor with Columns** (XII) with Flemish paintings, the **Room of Justice** (XIII) with portraits by **Titian, Veronese** and **Tintoretto; Flora's Room** (XIV) with paintings by **Andrea del Sarto, Bronzino** and **Pontormo;** the **Room of Putti** (XV) with Flemish paintings; the **Poccetti Gallery** (XVI), so called after the painter who decorated it, and which contains works by **Rubens, Dughet, Spagnoletto** and **Salvator Rosa**; The **Music** or **Drum Room,** (XVII) in neo-classical style with columns at the ends and, in the centre, a table in Russian malachite and gilded bronze; the **Castagnoli Room**

Filippo Lippi: Madonna with Child.

Tiziano: Portrait of a Gentleman, detail.

(XVIII) with the beautiful round table, known as the table of *Apollo and the Muses,* an outstanding work by the Semi-precious Stones Workshop; the **Apartment of the Allegories** by **Volterrano** (XIX-XXIII), so called after the artist who decorated the first room with frescoes dedicated to Vittoria della Rovere. In other rooms there are works by **Cigoli, Poccetti, Empoli, Allori** and **Salvator Rosa.**

8 ROYAL APARTMENTS - These are on the right hand side of the first floor of the Palace; access is through the *Room of the Niches.* At one time residence of the Medici and Lorraine families, it later became the representative home of the Savoy family. They make up a group of very fine rooms, re-opened to the public in 1993 after careful restoration work and search for the precious materials which had been dispersed, recomposing it in accordance with the Savoyard inventory of 1911, so as to offer the visitor a sumptuous display of three centuries of the history of furnishings: from the most interesting works in semi-precious stones made by Florentine craftsmen, to those of baroque, neo-classical and Art Nouveau styles. Worthy of special note are the *Throne Room.* with frescoes by G. Castagnoli and P. Sarti, the *White Room* and the *Oval Room,* also known as the Queen's dressing-room, with elegant eighteenth-century stuccoes. The numerous paintings and portraits of historical figures, particularly those by Sustermans, are also of interest.

70

Palatine Gallery: Throne-Room (Royal Apartments).

Palatine Gallery: The Queen's Room (Royal Apartments).

9 **SILVER MUSEUM** - One enters through the left corner of the courtyard. Founded in 1919, it houses a very rich collection of objects wrought in precious metals, semi-precious stones, porcelain and jewels, which were part of other treasures of the Medici and Hapsburg-Lorraine families. Of great importance is the collection of *vases made of semi-precious stones* belonging to Lorenzo the Magnificent, the Medici collection of *cameos and gems;* the beautiful rock crystal *casket* with Scenes from the Passion cut by Valerio Billi and the jewels of Anna Maria Ludovica Medici with pearls and precious stones set in gold.

10 **MUSEUM OF HISTORICAL CARRIAGES** - In the right wing of the Palace, it houses historical coaches and carriages of the nineteenth and twentieth centuries.

11 **MODERN ART GALLERY** - Situated on the second floor of the Palace. Founded by the Provisional Government in 1860, it has been further enriched with works from the Tuscan School of the nineteenth and twentieth centuries. The first rooms, dedicated to the neo-classical period, house paintings and sculptures by the best known artists of the time, including **Antonio Canova**, **Lorenzo Bartolini** and **Vincenzo Camuccini**. They are followed by rooms dedicated to Romantic art with paintings by **Francesco Hayez**, **Luigi Sabatelli**, **Antonio Fontanesi**, **Domenico Induno**, by the statesman **Massimo d'Azeglio**, and sculptures by **Amos Cassioli** and **Giovanni Duprè**.
Other rooms are dedicated to the Tuscan Purists and to historical and genre art; others, recently rearranged and enriched, are dedicated to the "Macchiaioli" (Florentine Impressionists) i.e., to the trend which grew in Tuscany in the second half of the nineteenth century marking the renewal of Italian art. In these rooms one can admire, arranged in groups, just as they were

Giovanni Fattori: Tuscany Maremma, detail.

Pitti Palace: view from the Boboli Garden.

offered by the collectors: works by **Giovanni Fattori** (1825-1908), the principal representative of "Macchia" painting, by **Silvestro Lega, Telemaco Signorini, Giuseppe de Nittis**. Of particular importance are the works of the legate of Diego Martelli, Benefactor of the "Macchiaioli"; the last rooms are dedicated to Italian contemporary art and house works by **Severini, Soffici, De Chirico, Casorati, Rosai, Romanelli** and **Marini**.

BOBOLI GARDENS A typical example of an Italian-style garden in which nature and architecture merge into a single artistic expression. It stretches up the Boboli hill, offering a superb panoramic view over the city and its surroundings and is enhanced by statues, fountains, grottoes, an amphitheatre and long avenues, commissioned by Cosimo I and Eleanor of Toledo. The garden is the product of the genius of five architects. Created by **Ammannati** from design by **Tribolo** (1549), it was continued by **Buontalenti** and completed by **Giulio** and **Alfonso Parigi**. **12**

PORCELAIN MUSEUM (Boboli Gardens - Casino del Cavaliere) - A priceless collection of various origins: Capodimonte, Sèvres, Chantilly, Vienna, Berlin, Worcester and China. It was housed in the present museum, known as the *Casino del Cavaliere,* (built by Cosimo III) in 1973, and groups together porcelain from the Silver Museum in three rooms. **13**

14 **SPECOLA MUSEUM** (17, via Romana) - This *Physics and Natural History Museum,* once an Astronomy and Meteorology Observatory, was founded by the Grand Duke Peter Leopold of Lorraine to house, amongst other things, scientific material left by the Medici family. The outstanding collection of *anatomical figures in coloured wax* is the work of Cigoli and the Siciliani, Michele and Gaetano Zumbo, but above of all, by Susini, Calamai and Calenzuoli.

15 **CHURCH OF SANTO SPIRITO** (piazza S. Spirito) - Begun by **Brunelleschi** in 1444 and continued by Manetti, it is one of the purest creations of the early Renaissance period. The *Dome,* designed by Brunelleschi, is the work of **Salvi di Andrea** (1481) and the *Bell Tower* is by **Baccio d'Agnolo** (1517). The *interior,* a Latin cross with a nave and two aisles, reflects the linear perspective typical of Brunelleschi's architecture, based on harmony of proportions and spaces. Of particular interest is the *Vestibule* by **Cronaca** (1494) and the *Sacristy* by **Giuliano da Sangallo** (1492) to which the *Crucifixion,* a juvenile work by **Michelangelo,** has been returned. To the left of the church, in the building housing the *Salvatore Romano Foundation,* one can admire the *Last Supper* frescoed by **Orcagna** around 1360. This important church is situated at the end of the picturesque Piazza Santo Spirito. At no. 10 of this square there is the sixteenth-century *Palazzo Guadagni*, also erected by **Cronaca.**

Brunelleschi: Church of the Holy Spirit - Interior.

74

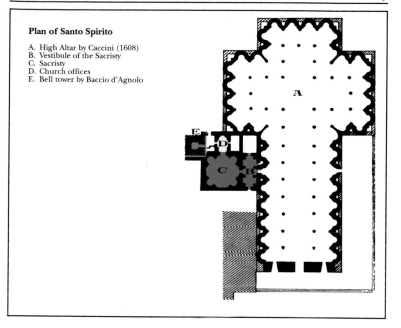

Plan of Santo Spirito

A. High Altar by Caccini (1608)
B. Vestibule of the Sacristy
C. Sacristy
D. Church offices
E. Bell tower by Baccio d'Agnolo

CHURCH OF THE CARMINE (piazza del Carmine) - Built during the Roman-Gothic period, it was almost entirely destroyed by fire in 1771 and completely rebuilt in the eighteenth century. The *interior* is in the form of a Latin cross with a single nave and false architectural perspectives in the vault painted by Domenico Stagi. At the end of the right transept is the ***Brancacci Chapel***, miraculously spared by the fire, with the famous series of frescoes depicting *Scenes from the life of St. Peter* and the *Original Sin* and whose restoration, carried out using advanced techniques and scrupulous precision in 1984 has, after centuries, led to a new interpretation. Begun by **Masolino** (1424-25), continued by **Masaccio** (1425-28) and finished by **Filippino Lippi** (1481-85), these frescoes are amongst the masterpieces of Italian painting. Particularly worthy of note are those attributed to **Masaccio**, who with his works marked the beginning of Florentine Renaissance painting, of which he then became one of the major exponents. Securely attributed to him are: *Expulsion from the Garden of Eden, Paying of Tribute Money, St Peter and St John giving Alms, St Peter healing the Sick with his Shadow, St Peter on his Throne, St Peter baptising the Neophytes.* In the centre, above the altar, is the panel of the *Madonna del Carmine,* also known as the *Madonna of the People,* of the Tuscan school of the second half of the thirteenth century (attributed to **Coppo di Marcovaldo**). Amongst the Church's many later works, is the ***Corsini Chapel,*** with frescoes by **Luca Giordano** in the left transept. The Vestibule, next to the Brancacci Chapel, leads to the fifteenth-century ***Sacristy***, housing works by **Andrea da Firenze**, and to the small ***Chapel*** with frescoes by **Bicci di Lorenzo.** From the Sacristy one enters the great seventeenth-century ***Cloister*** which looks over the ***Refectory*** frescoed by **Allori** (1582).

16

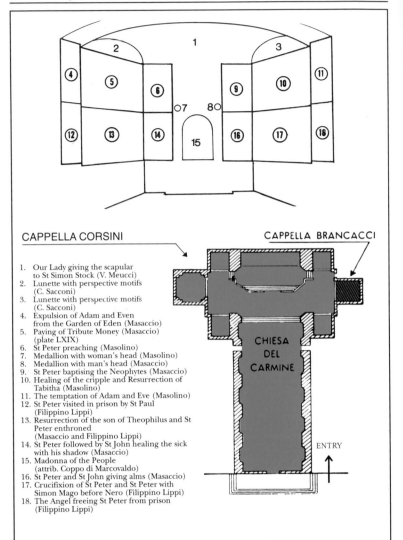

CAPPELLA CORSINI

CAPPELLA BRANCACCI

1. Our Lady giving the scapular to St Simon Stock (V. Meucci)
2. Lunette with perspective motifs (C. Sacconi)
3. Lunette with perspective motifs (C. Sacconi)
4. Expulsion of Adam and Even from the Garden of Eden (Masaccio)
5. Paying of Tribute Money (Masaccio) (plate LXIX)
6. St Peter preaching (Masolino)
7. Medallion with woman's head (Masolino)
8. Medallion with man's head (Masaccio)
9. St Peter baptising the Neophytes (Masaccio)
10. Healing of the cripple and Resurrection of Tabitha (Masolino)
11. The temptation of Adam and Eve (Masolino)
12. St Peter visited in prison by St Paul (Filippino Lippi)
13. Resurrection of the son of Theophilus and St Peter enthroned (Masaccio and Filippino Lippi)
14. St Peter followed by St John healing the sick with his shadow (Masaccio)
15. Madonna of the People (attrib. Coppo di Marcovaldo)
16. St Peter and St John giving alms (Masaccio)
17. Crucifixion of St Peter and St Peter with Simon Mago before Nero (Filippino Lippi)
18. The Angel freeing St Peter from prison (Filippino Lippi)

CHIESA DEL CARMINE

ENTRY

Masaccio: The Tribute, detail.

Masaccio: The expulsion of Adam and Eve, detail.

CHURCH OF SAN FREDIANO IN CESTELLO (4, via di Cestello) - **17**
The church is in the heart of San Frediano, the old and
characteristic Medieval district of "Oltrarno" (left bank of the
Arno), still full of artisans workshops and teeming with local colour.
Formerly St Maria degli Angeli, it was rebuilt between 1680-89 by
Antonio Maria Ferri to a design by Cerutti. The impressive dome
vault with cylindrical drum is also by Ferri. The baroque interior is
decorated with frescoes by Gabbiani and Curradi.

FOURTH ITINERARY

1 PIAZZA SAN FIRENZE
2 BARGELLO PALACE
3 BARGELLO NATIONAL
  MUSEUM
4 CHURCH OF THE BADIA
  FIORENTINA
5 HOUSE OF DANTE
6 HOUSE OF BUONARROTI
7 PIAZZA SANTA CROCE

8 BASILICA OF SANTA CROCE
9 MUSEUM OF SANTA CROCE
  CHURCH
10 PAZZI CHAPEL
11 HORNE MUSEUM
12 BARDINI MUSEUM-
   CORSI GALLERY
13 SCIENCE HISTORY MUSEUM

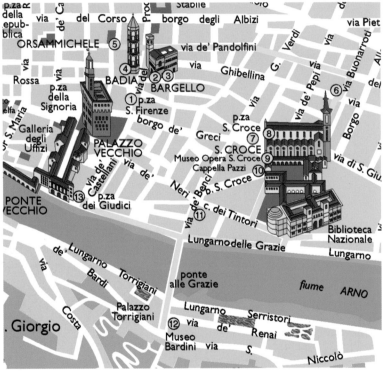

1 PIAZZA SAN FIRENZE - A suggestive and harmonious square dominated by the baroque façade of the ancient *Philippine Convent of St Firenze*, built in 1715 by **Ruggeri** and now seat of the Law Courts. Opposite is *Palazzo Gondi* built by **Giuliano da Sangallo** in 1494, a splendid example of a noble residence in which Leonardo da Vinci also lived; to its right stands the fine Gothic *bell tower* of the *Badia*, contrasted by the crenellated tower of the majestic *Bargello Palace*.

2 BARGELLO PALACE - Begun in 1255, as the residence of the Captain of the People, it was extended in later years and completed around the middle of the fourteenth century. The tower, known as the "Volognana", incorporated in the palace, was built in 1255. From 1261 it was the seat of the Podestà and, from 1502, of the Council of Justice. In 1574 the Bargello (Captain of Justice) established himself there and during this period it was turned into a

78

Bargello: Exterior with the Volognona tower.

grim prison with torture and execution chambers. After restoration by **Francesco Mazzei** in 1865 the Palace was restored to its former splendour and is now considered a fine example of Florentine Gothic architecture.

Inside, in the suggestive and picturesque asymmetrical *courtyard*, is an original external staircase by **Neri di Fioravant**i (1367), leading to the elegant arched loggia on the first floor. Today the Palace houses the *Bargello National Museum*.

BARGELLO NATIONAL MUSEUM - (4, via del Proconsolo) - **3**
Founded in 1859, this Museum is of fundamental importance owing to its priceless collection of Tuscan Renaissance sculptures, and very rich collection of antique objects and arms. From the Vestibule one enters the very large *Hall* (I), which houses **Michelangelo's** early works; *Drunken Bacchus* (1499), a marble tondo of the *Madonna with Child* and *St Giovannino* (1504), *David* or *Apollino* (circa 1531), a *Bust of Brutus* (1504); as well as sculptures by **Daniele da Volterra**, **Jacopo Sansovino**, **Giambologna**, **Ammannati**, **Bandinelli**, **Bernini** and a *Bust of Cosimo I* by **Benvenuto Cellini**. After crossing the courtyard under the portico opposite the entrance, one passes through two *Rooms*, one (II) exhibits International Gothic works and the other (III) contains sculptures from the Tuscan school of the fourteenth century (*Madonna with Child* by **Tino da Camaino**).

1st Floor - In the *Loggia* there are bronze sculptures and statues by **Giambologna**, including *Mercury*, two putti and a satyr. The *General Council Room* (I) is dedicated to the sculpture of the first half of the fifteenth century and in particular to **Donatello**. His works include: *St George* (1416), *David* in bronze (1430), *St Giovannino*; besides these, one can admire sculptures by **Desiderio da Settignano, Brunelleschi, Ghiberti, Bertoldo, Agostino di Duccio, Luca della Robbia** and **Michelozzo.** There follow: the *Room of the Tower* (II), and the *Room of the Podestà* (III), which house tapestries, materials, carpets and gold work, enamels and various objects from the thirteenth to the sixteenth century; a little further on is the *Podestà Chapel* (IV), with frescoes, in very poor condition, by **Giotto** and the *Sacristy* (V). From the Room of the Podestà one passes to the *Ivories Room* (VI) with polychrome wooden statues of the fourteenth and fifteenth-century Tuscan school. then follow the *Goldsmithery Room* (VII) and the *Majolica Room* (VIII), with works from ancient workshops in Florence, Siena, Faenza, Urbino and Gubbio.

2nd Floor - One enters the *Room* (I) dedicated to **Giovanni della Robbia**, containing the artist's terracotta works and those from his workshop. In *Room* (II), known as the *"Room with the Washbasin"*, glazed terracotta by **Andrea della Robbia**; in *Room* (III) sculptures

Donatello: David in bronze.   *Michelangelo: Bacchus.*

Andrea della Robbia: Young Boy.

by **Verrocchio,** including the famous *David* in bronze and *Lady Mazzolino,* in addition to works by **Antonio del Pollaiolo** (*Hercules and Antaeus*), **Antonio Rossellino, Benedetto da Maiano** and **Mino da Fiesole**. From here one continues to the *Fireplace Room* (VI) where there is an important collection of small Renaissance bronzes and a magnificent stone *fireplace*, a work by **Benedetto da Rovezzano**. Again from *Room* (III) one can reach the smaller *Rooms* (IV) and (V), where there is a very fine collection of Medicean medals of the fifteenth and sixteenth century. Finally, *Room* (VII) has a magnificent collection of *arms and armour* and *Room* (VIII) houses cloths from the *Franchetti collection*.

CHURCH OF THE BADIA FIORENTINA (4, via Condotta) - An ancient Benedictine Abbey that dates to the tenth century which was extended in Cistercian Gothic style in the fourteenth century. The interior was completely rebuilt by Matteo Segaloni in 1627. The remarkable portal by **Benedetto da Rovezzano** (1495) is surmounted by a *Madonna with Child* in glazed terracotta by **Buglioni**. In the baroque *interior,* shaped like a Greek cross, one can admire various sculptures by **Mino da Fiesole** (*Madonna with Child*

81

and *St Lawrence and St Leonard* in bas-relief; the *tombs* of Bernardo Giugni and Count Ugo, fine examples of Renaissance sepulchral monuments) and a painting on wood (*The Virgin appearing to St. Bernard*) by **Filippino Lippi**. From the **Cloister of the Oranges** by **Rossellino** (1435-40), frescoed with *Stories from St Benedict* (detached from the wall) one can enjoy a suggestive view of the fine hexagonal bell tower.

Continuing along Via Proconsolo one comes to *Palazzo Nonfinito*, once owned by the Strozzi family, which was begun in 1593 but never finished. Today it houses *National Museum of Anthropology and Ethnology*, the first of its kind in Italy, founded in 1869 by Paolo Mantegazza.

5 **HOUSE OF DANTE** (1, via S. Margherita) - Rebuilt between 1875 and 1910 on the ruins of the ancient house which probably belonged to the Alighieri family, the so-called Casa di Dante houses mementos of Dante and contemporary painting exhibitions. Next to it is the medieval *Torre della Castagna*, first residence of the Art Priors. In the same road stands the little church of *St Margherita dei Cerchi*, where Dante is said to have met Beatrice.

6 **HOUSE OF BUONARROTI** (70, via Gibellina) - Bought by Michelangelo for his nephew Leonardo and later decorated by Leonardo's son, Michelangelo the Younger, in the seventeenth century, it was left to the city of Florence in 1858 by the last descendant of the Buonarroti family. The following year it was turned into a *Museum* to house some of **Michelangelo**'s early works; two bas-reliefs: the *Madonna of the Stairs* (1490 -1492), his first known sculpture and the *Battle of the Centaurs* (1492); a model of a

Michelangelo: Madonna of the Stairs, detail.

river divinity for the Medicean Chapel; various models in earthenware, wax and wood and a rich collection of his drawings. The museum also houses a series of portraits depicting Michelangelo, sculptures portraying members of his family and the archaeological and coin collection of the Buonarroti family.

PIAZZA SANTA CROCE - This is a historical square, dating to Medieval times, where the people held their meetings. During the Renaissance tournaments took place here, like the famous joust of Giuliano de' Medici, immortalised by the verses of Poliziano. Even today the square is the heart of the ancient and characteristic Santa Croce district, where the traditional football game in costume is played. Among the ancient *palaces* which overlook the square are the fifteenth-century *Palazzo dei Serristori,* attributed to **Baccio d'Agnolo** and *Palazzo dell'Antella* by **Parigi** (1619), with polychrome decorations on the façade painted by the followers of Giovanni da San Giovanni. The square is however dominated by the *Church of Santa Croce.* **7**

BASILICA OF SANTA CROCE - Begun in 1294 to a design allegedly by **Arnolfo di Cambio**, this Franciscan basilica is one of the finest expressions of Florentine Gothic architecture. The *bell tower* (1874) by **Baccani** and the marble *façade* (1845-63) by **Matas**, in strong contrast to the sobriety of the building, date back to the last century. The spacious interior has a classical serenity. Shaped like an Egyptian cross, it is divided into three immense and luminous naves with octagonal pilasters and is covered by a open **8**

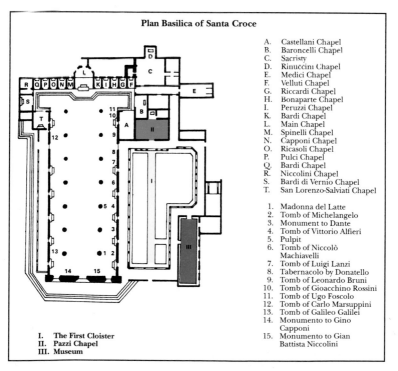

Plan Basilica of Santa Croce

A. Castellani Chapel
B. Baroncelli Chapel
C. Sacristy
D. Rinuccini Chapel
E. Medici Chapel
F. Velluti Chapel
G. Riccardi Chapel
H. Bonaparte Chapel
I. Peruzzi Chapel
K. Bardi Chapel
L. Main Chapel
M. Spinelli Chapel
N. Capponi Chapel
O. Ricasoli Chapel
P. Pulci Chapel
Q. Bardi Chapel
R. Niccolini Chapel
S. Bardi di Vernio Chapel
T. San Lorenzo-Salviati Chapel

1. Madonna del Latte
2. Tomb of Michelangelo
3. Monument to Dante
4. Tomb of Vittorio Alfieri
5. Pulpit
6. Tomb of Niccolò Machiavelli
7. Tomb of Luigi Lanzi
8. Tabernacolo by Donatello
9. Tomb of Leonardo Bruni
10. Tomb of Gioacchino Rossini
11. Tomb of Ugo Foscolo
12. Tomb of Carlo Marsuppini
13. Tomb of Galileo Galilei
14. Monumento to Gino Capponi
15. Monumento to Gian Battista Niccolini

I. The First Cloister
II. Pazzi Chapel
III. Museum

Basilica of S. Croce.

Interior of the Basilica of S. Croce.

84

Donatello: The Annunciation.

trussed wooden ceiling. Here one can admire the funeral monuments of important personalities and works of great artistic interest.

Internal façade - *Monument to Gino Capponi*, a nineteenth-century Florentine humanist, by A. Bortone (1884); *Monument to G. B. Niccolini*, poet and historian of the last century, by Pio Fedi (1883).

Central nave - At the third pilaster on the right is a splendid *pulpit* by **Benedetto da Maiano** (circa 1475) depicting *Scenes from the life of St Francis*; at the last pilaster on the left there is a *Monument to Leon Battista Alberti* with statue by Lorenzo Bartolini (1840-50).

Right Nave - At the first altar: *Crucifixion* by **Santi di Tito**. *Monument to Michelangelo Buonarroti* by **Vasari** and assistants (1570) with the allegorical figures of Painting, Sculpture and Architecture; on the opposite pilaster, an exquisite almond-shaped alto-rilievo of the *Madonna with Child* by **Antonio Rossellino**; at the second altar: *On the way to Calvary* by **Vasari**; *Cenotaph of Dante Alighieri*, work of **Stefano Ricci** dated 1825 (the poet's tomb is in Ravenna where Dante died in exile in 1321); *Monument to Vittorio Alfieri*, work of **Canova** (1810) with the allegorical figure of Italy in sorrow; *Monument to Niccolò Machiavelli* by **Innocenzo Spinazzi** (1787) with the allegorical figure Diplomacy, holding in its hand a Tondo on which the Statesman is portrayed; a stone *Tabernacle* representing the *Annunciation*, an important work by **Donatello** (circa 1435); Tomb of the historian and humanist Leonardo Bruni (1444) by **Bernardo Rossellino**; *Monument to Gioacchino Rossini* by **Cassioli**; at the sixth altar: *Entry of Jesus into Jerusalem* by **Cigoli**; in addition, the *Monument to Ugo Foscolo*, the poet who immortalised the tombs of

85

Santa Croce in the poem *"The Sepulchres"*, a work by **Berti** (1939).
Right arm of the transept: The *Castellani Chapel* with frescoes by
Agnolo and **Taddeo Gaddi** depicting stories of *St Nicholas of Bari, St
Anthony Abbot* and *John the Baptist* (circa 1385); the *Baroncelli Chapel*
painted by **Taddeo Gaddi** in 1332-38, with *Stories from the life of the
Virgin*. On the altar is a painting of the *Coronation of the Virgin*, by
Giotto's workshop. On the wall at the end on the right: *Madonna of
the Belt* by **Sebastiano Mainardi**, a pupil of Ghirlandaio. This is
followed by the fourteenth-century *Sacristy* with frescoes by **Taddeo
Gaddi** and **Niccolò Gerini** and, in the same Sacristy, the *Rinuccini
Chapel,* frescoed by **Giovanni da Milano** with *Stories of Mary Magdalen*
and *Stories of the Virgin*; at the end of the corridor is the *Medici
Chapel* by **Michelozzo**, on the altar a terracotta *Madonna with Child*
by **Andrea della Robbia**. Returning to the church, the *Velluti Chapel*,
the *Calderini Riccardi Chapel* with its vault frescoed by **Giovanni da
San Giovanni** and the *Giugni Chapel* with the Buonaparte Tombs
(Carlotta's Tomb is by Bartolini).
And so to the *Peruzzi Chapel* (1320) with frescoes by **Giotto**
depicting *Stories of St John the Baptist* and *St John the Evangelist* and
hence to the *Bardi Chapel,* again painted entirely by **Giotto** (1317)
with *Episodes from the Life of St Francis,* fundamental works of Italian
Art. Thereafter, the *Main Chapel* with the *Legend of the Cross,*
frescoed by **Agnolo Gaddi** (circa 1380); on the altar the triptych by

Vasari: Monument to Michelangelo Buonarroti.

Giotto: Bardi Chapel - The Death of Saint Francis.

Niccolò Gerini and the *Crucifix* of the so-called "Maestro of Figline", and the *Tosinghi Chapel* once frescoed by Giotto. One then comes to the *Capponi Chapel* and the *Ricasoli Chapel*, completely restored in the nineteenth century, with paintings by Sabatelli; from here to the *Bardi di Libertà Chapel* with frescoes by **Bernardo Daddi** and *altar-piece* by **Giovanni della Robbia**. This right arm of the cross-vault closes with the *Bardi di Vernio Chapel,* decorated by **Maso di Banco** with *Stories of St Silvester* (circa 1340).

Left arm of the transept: *Niccolini Chapel* with frescoes by **Volterrano** on the vault. Of particular interest is the *Bardi Chapel* with the famous *Crucifix* by **Donatello.** In the *Salviati Chapel* is the tomb of the Countess Sofia Somoyski Czartoryski, sculpted by Lorenzo Bartolini. On the left: *Monument to Luigi Cherubini.*

Left Nave: At the sixth altar: *Pentecost* by **Vasari**; *Monument to the humanist Carlo Marsuppini*, Secretary of the Florentine Republic, by **Desiderio da Settignano**; at the fifth altar: *Ascension* by **Stradano**; on the walls between the fifth and fourth altars, *Pietà* by **Bronzino**: on the floor, memorial stone of Lorenzo and Vittorio Ghiberti; at the fourth altar, *the Doubting of St Thomas* by **Vasari** and on the third altar: *Supper in Emmaus* by Santi di Tito; at the second altar, again by **Santi di Tito:** *Resurrection;* a little further on is the *Monument to Galileo Galilei* by Foggini, with the allegorical figures of Astrology and Geometry.

MUSEUM OF SANTA CROCE CHURCH (16, piazza Santa Croce) - **9** In the cloister leading to the convent, on the left is the *Santa Croce Church Museum*, housed in the ancient *Refectory* and adjoining rooms. It has an interesting collection of Florentine paintings and sculptures dating from the fourteenth to the sixteenth century: the well-known *Crucifix* by **Cimabue** (badly damaged in the 1966 flood); *St Ludwig* in bronze (1423) by **Donatello** and other works by **Maso di Banco**, **Orcagna**, **Bicci di Lorenzo**, **Domenico Veneziano** and **Bronzino**. On the wall at the back of the Refectory one can admire the *Tree of the Cross* and the *Last Supper*, detached frescoes, by **Taddeo Gaddi**.

Sacristy: Taddeo Gaddi - Life of Jesus, detail.

10 **PAZZI CHAPEL** (16, piazza Santa Croce) - To the right of the church at the back of the fourteenth-century cloister, stands one of **Brunelleschi's** most graceful and harmonious works: the *Pazzi Chapel,* where Renaissance spaces are rhythmically divided by the structure both inside and outside the chapel. At the front is a pronaos made up of six stone columns which support a high attic: the frieze is decorated with medallions sculptured by **Desiderio da Settignano**. From the roof an impressive cylindrical dome emerges, surmounted by a slender lantern. In the interior the *tondi* and *rose ornaments* in polychrome terracotta are by **Luca della Robbia** and his workshops. Brunelleschi, commissioned to work on the Chapel by Andrea Pazzi, devoted himself to this work from 1443 to 1446, the year in which he died, leaving the original façade unfinished.
Not far from piazza Santa Croce, at no.1, piazza Cavalleggeri, is the *Biblioteca Nazionale* (National Library), one of the most important libraries in Italy. It suffered a great deal of damage during the 1966 flood.

11 **HORNE MUSEUM** (6, via dei Benci) - A splendid late fifteenth-century palace, possibly the work of Cronaca, it houses a small but important museum of furniture and antique objects, but above all paintings. Some of the most important are: *St Stephen* by **Giotto**; *Crucifixion* and *Madonna with Four Saints* by **Bernardo Daddi**; *Three Saints* by **Pietro Lorenzetti**; *St Sebastian* by **Ercole Roberti**; *Holy Family* by **Beccafumi**; *Allegory of Music* by **Dosso Dossi**; *Pietà* by **Filippo Lippi**. Also important is the collection of *drawings* by **Michelangelo, Raphael, Andrea del Sarto, Carracci, Poussin** and other of great painters of the eighteenth-century Venetian School.
A little further on, at the corner with Borgo Santa Croce, is a typical

Brunelleschi: Cloisters with the Pazzi Chapel.

Florentine tower-house, once the property of the Alberti family with a small fifteenth-century loggia in front.

Opposite the Horne Museum, at no. 5, is the *Bardi-Serzelli Palace*, reputed to be the work of Brunelleschi's youth: In this palace, where, at the end of the sixteenth century the *Camerata fiorentina* had its headquarters, Melodrama originated.

From Via dei Benci one arrives at the modern **Ponte alle Grazie**. Built in 1237 and, like the other bridges of Florence, small claustral cells were built in it, in one of which lived St Apollonia. The bridge was destroyed during the last war and subsequently rebuilt.

BARDINI MUSEUM, CORSI GALLERY (1, piazza dei Mozzi) - **12** Housed in a nineteenth-century building, it contains the collection left to the city by the antiquarian Stefano Bardini in 1922. It comprises a rich collection of furniture, ceramics, arms, medals, tapestries, carpets, paintings and sculptures (the most of important of which is *Charity* by **Tino da Camaino**).

On the first floor of the building is the Corsi Gallery, where 60 works of art from various schools from 1100 to 1800 are exhibited.

SCIENCE HISTORY MUSEUM (1, piazza dei Giudici) - In the **13** medieval *Palazzo Castellani*, seat of the Rota Judges from 1574 to 1841, is the Museum of History and Science founded in 1930 to house scientific instruments from Medici and private collections and from the Arcispedale di Santa Maria Nuova collection. Some of the most interesting exhibits are **Galileo's** *lens* and *compass* and **Torricelli's** *barometer.*

FIFTH ITINERARY

5

1 PIAZZA DELLA SANTISSIMA ANNUNZIATA
2 INNOCENTI PORTICO AND FOUNDLING HOSPITAL
3 BASILICA OF SANTISSIMA ANNUNZIATA
4 ARCHEOLOGICAL MUSEUM

5 CHURCH OF SANTA MARIA MADDALENA DE' PAZZI
6 JEWISH TEMPLE
7 PERGOLA THEATRE
8 HISTORICAL AND TOPOGRAPHIC MUSEUM "FLORENCE IN OLDEN TIMES"

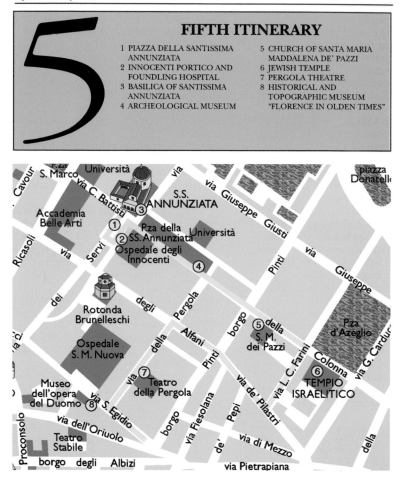

1 PIAZZA DELLA SANTISSIMA ANNUNZIATA - The serenity and elegance of its architecture and the sense of space make this a splendid example of a Renaissance square. It is surrounded by *porticoes* on three sides; that of the *Church of the Santissima Annunziata* at the end, that of the *Confraternity dei Servi di Maria*, work of **Antonio da Sangallo** and **Baccio d'Agnolo** (1525), on the left; on the right the portico of the *Ospedale degli Innocenti* (1419-26) by **Brunelleschi**. Between the portico of the Confraternity and Via dei Servi is *Palazzo Grifoni* (1563) by **Ammannati**. The *equestrian statue* of Grand Duke Ferdinand I which stands in the centre of the square, was begun by **Giambologna** and finished by **Tacca** in 1608; the two bronze *fountains* at either side are by **Tacca** and his assistants (1629).

2 INNOCENTI PORTICO AND FOUNDLING HOSPITAL (Ospedale degli Innocenti) - One of the oldest institutions in Europe for abandoned children, it was designed by **Brunelleschi** in 1419 and finished in 1445 by Francesco della Luna. The building, which stands on the top of a flight of steps, has a *portico* in front with nine great arcades on slender columns: the ten ceramic *medallions* decorating the spandrels are by **Andrea della Robbia**. Inside, in the

90

portico of the central cloister is a terracotta lunette representing the *Annunciation*, again by **Andrea della Robbia**. On the first floor, in the corridors overlooking the cloister, is a *collection of sinopias and frescoes* of the Florentine school between the fourteenth and seventeenth centuries. A Hall houses the *Hospital Gallery* with paintings by **Botticelli** and **Ghirlandaio** and sculptures by **Luca della Robbia, Benedetto da Maiano** and **Antonio Rossellino**.

BASILICA OF SANTISSIMA ANNUNZIATA - Erected in 1250 and completely rebuilt in the fifteenth century by **Michelozzo**, it was restored in later centuries. It has a seventeenth-century portico in front through which one enters the *Chiostrino dei Voti*, rebuilt by **Manetti** from a design by Michelozzo and decorated with frescoes by **Pontormo, Andrea del Sarto**, **Rosso Fiorentino** and other well-known Tuscan mannerists. **3**

The baroque *interior* has a single nave: on the left as one enters is a small elegant Renaissance *temple* (1447-61) after a design by **Michelozzo** for the miraculous image of Our Lady of the Annunciation on the altar. The adjacent *Feroni Chapel,* by **Foggini** (1692), is a rare example of baroque sculpture and architecture in Florence. Positioned above the altar is the *Saviour and St Julian,* a fresco by **Andrea del Castagno**.

The other side chapels contain important works by **Perugino, Bernardo Rossellino** and again by **Andrea del Castagno**. The great circular tribune by **Michelozzo** is covered by the original semispherical dome designed by **Leon Battista Alberti** (1444). In the adjoining *Cloister of the Dead,* also by **Michelozzo**, one can admire frescoes by **Poccetti** and **Matteo Rosselli** and the *Madonna with Sack* by **Andrea del Sarto**. On the northern side of the cloister is the *Chapel of the Confraternity of St. Luke* (home of the ancient Academy of Drawing Arts) where Cellini, Pontormo and other great

View of the Church of SS. Annunziata and the Hospital of the Innocents.

artists are buried; works by **Antonio Sangallo, Luca Giordano, Vasari, Bronzino** and **Santi di Tito** are also preserved here.

ARCHEOLOGICAL MUSEUM (38, via della Colonna) - This Museum is housed in *Palazzo della Crocetta,* built in 1620 by **Parigi** for the Grand Duchess Mary Magdalen of Austria. **4**
It was founded in 1870 and is particularly important for its

The Chimera, Etruscan bronze from the 5th - 4th century B.C.

testimonies to Etruscan civilisation. It is arranged as follows:
Ground Floor: *Greek, Etruscan and Roman sculptures* (Artemis
Laphria); *Etrurian Topographic Museum* (in the garden Etruscan
tombs and funeral monuments).
First Floor: *Egyptian Museum*, one of the most important in the
world; *Etruscan, Greek and Roman Antiquarium* with sculptures and
small Etruscan, Greek and Roman bronzes (the *Haranguer*, the
Chimera of Arezzo and the *Small Idol); Numismatic Room and Collection
of Precious objects*, glass, gold and silverware.
Second Floor: A continuation of the *Antiquarium* and *Prehistoric
Section*, with objects from Tuscany; other rooms are dedicated to
Italic and eastern Mediterranean finds, a collection of clay and
terracotta objects (*Vase François*), and paintings from the tombs of
Orvieto which have been transferred on to canvas. Also on the
second floor is a collection of Etruscan plaster casts.

5 **CHURCH OF SANTA MARIA MADDALENA DE' PAZZI** (58, Borgo
Pinti) - This church was founded together with the adjacent
Benedictine Monastery in the thirteenth century and renovated
several times, notably by **Giuliano da Sangallo,** who was also
responsible for the spacious trabecular *courtyard* in front of the
church. The huge Renaissance interior was restored in the
seventeenth and eighteenth centuries; the paintings in the chapels,
like those by Ciro Ferri on the dome of the *Main Chapel* and the two

canvases with *Stories of Mary Magdalen* by **Luca Giordano,** also date back to that period. In the *Chapter Room* in the adjoining convent, worthy of note are the frescoes by **Perugino** painted between 1494 and 1496, designed as though seen through three different arches: through the central arch a view of the *Crucifixion and Mary Magdalen*, to the left *St Bernard and Mary*, and to the right *St John the Evangelist and St Benedict*.

THE JEWISH TEMPLE (4, via Farini) - Built thanks to the legacy of David Levi, who bequeathed his patrimony to build a "monumental Temple worthy of Florence". The *Synagogue*, built by the architects **M. Treves, M. Falcini** and **V. Micheli** (1874-82), in Moorish style, is topped by an immense hemispheric bronze dome. The exterior is characterised by suggestive polychromy stonework, while the interior is entirely frescoed and decorated with Venetian mosaics. In the courtyard huge marble tombstones list the names of deported Jews who failed to return after the end of the war. Next to the Synagogue is the *Museum* which houses ancient manuscripts, parchments and furnishings relating to the Jewish religion. **6**

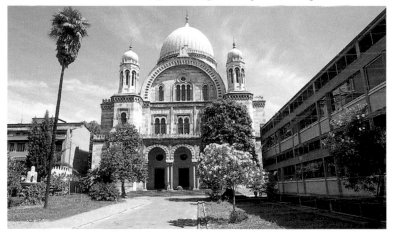

The Synagogue.

PERGOLA THEATRE (18, via della Pergola) - Built by **Ferdinando Tacca** in 1652, it is the first oval shaped theatre with the stalls placed one above the other. Mobile scenographic sets were experimented and approved in this theatre and subsequently used all over the world. **7**

HISTORICAL AND TOPOGRAPHIC MUSEUM FIRENZE COM'ERA (Florence in olden times) (21, via Sant' Egidio) The Museum is situated in the ancient *Convent of the Oblate Sisters*, in front of Santa Maria Nuova Hospital. It houses a rich collection of paintings, drawings, prints and photographs illustrating the evolution of the city from the fifteenth century up to the present day. The outstanding series of *lunettes* with views of Medicean Villas was painted in tempera by **Giusto Utens** in 1599. The Museum also houses a *permanent exhibition* by the Florentine painter **Ottone Rosai** (1895-1957). In the same building is the *Florentine Prehistory Museum* of weapons, artistic objects and casts of fossilised skulls of the Neolithic, Palaeolithic and Iron Ages, found during excavations and research in Italy and the rest of Europe. **8**

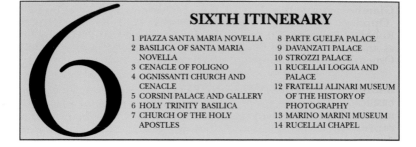

SIXTH ITINERARY

1 PIAZZA SANTA MARIA NOVELLA
2 BASILICA OF SANTA MARIA NOVELLA
3 CENACLE OF FOLIGNO
4 OGNISSANTI CHURCH AND CENACLE
5 CORSINI PALACE AND GALLERY
6 HOLY TRINITY BASILICA
7 CHURCH OF THE HOLY APOSTLES
8 PARTE GUELFA PALACE
9 DAVANZATI PALACE
10 STROZZI PALACE
11 RUCELLAI LOGGIA AND PALACE
12 FRATELLI ALINARI MUSEUM OF THE HISTORY OF PHOTOGRAPHY
13 MARINO MARINI MUSEUM
14 RUCELLAI CHAPEL

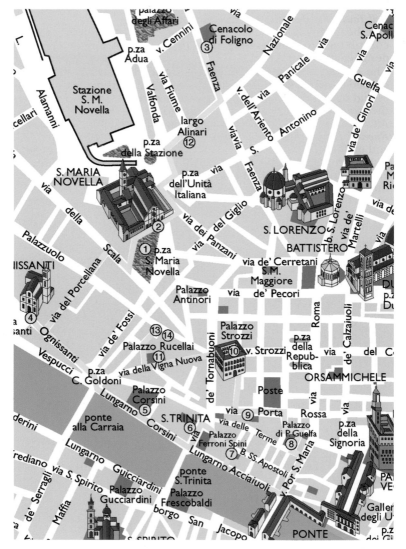

1 PIAZZA SANTA MARIA NOVELLA - An asymmetrical medieval square where the *"Palio dei Cocchi"* (Chariot Race), instituted by Cosimo I, used to take place. Even today the *obelisks* erected by

Giambologna remind us of the course covered by the race. Opposite the church is the ***Loggia of St Paul***, decorated with Robbian terracotta. Erected at the end of the fifteenth century, it is as an imitation of the Loggia built by Brunelleschi in front of the Ospedale degli Innocenti in Piazza Santissima Annunziata.

BASILICA OF SANTA MARIA NOVELLA - This famous Florentine basilica, with its clear proportions and concrete sense of space, is a masterpiece of fourteenth-century Gothic architecture. It represents the Dominican ideology: **Sisto** and **Ristoro,** who designed it in 1246 were, in fact, Dominican friars. Frá **Jacopo Talenti** da Nipozzano, also responsible for the *Sacristy* and the tall *Bell Tower*, finished the building in 1360.
The beautiful Romanesque-Gothic *façade* of the lower half was completed in Renaissance style in 1476 by **Alberti**, who also designed the central portal.
The *interior*, vast and harmonious, is shaped like an Egyptian cross, divided into a nave and two aisles by slender pilasters made up of arches and ogival vaults. It houses important works of art, among which: the *Crucifixion*, a juvenile work by **Giotto**, in the centre of the nave, *Monument to the Beata Villana* by **Bernardo Rossellino** (1451), the *Rucellai Chapel* with a *tomb slab* to Leonardo Dati by **Ghiberti** (1423) and on the altar, *Madonna with Child* by **Nino Pisano**; the *Strozzi Chapel* with frescoes by **Filippino Lippi** (1503) and the elegant marble *tomb* of Filippo Strozzi by **Benedetto da Maiano** (1441); The *Main Chapel* with the famous series of *frescoes* by **Domenico del Ghirlandaio** and his assistants (1485-90), and on the altar a bronze *Crucifix* by **Giambologna**; the Gondi Chapel with a *wooden Crucifix* by **Brunelleschi**, famous for the harmony of its proportions; the *Strozzi of Mantova Chapel* with fourteenth-century *frescoes* by **Nardo di Cione** (1357).

The Basilica of S. Maria Novella.

95

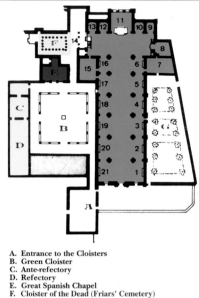

Plan of Church of Santa Maria Novella

1. Tomb of Sen. Ippolito Venturi (S. Ricci)
2. Monument of the Beata Villana (Bernardo Rossellino)
3. Presentation at the temple (Naldini, 1577)
4. Deposition (Naldini)
5. St Vincenzo Ferreri preaching (Iacopo del Meglio - 16th century)
6. St Raymond resurrecting a dead child (Iacopo Ligozzi)
7. Pura Chapel
8. Rucellai Chapel
9. Bardi Chapel
10. Strozzi Chapel
11. Main Chapel
12. Gondi Chapel
13. Gaddi Chapel
14. Strozzi Chapel
15. Sacristy
16. St Giacinto (Alessandro Allori)
17. St Caterina da Siena (Poccetti)
18. Resurrection (Vasari)
19. Trinity by Masaccio
20. The Samaritan at the Well (Alessandro Allori)
21. Resurrection of Lazarus (Santi di Tito)

A. Entrance to the Cloisters
B. Green Cloister
C. Ante-refectory
D. Refectory
E. Great Spanish Chapel
F. Cloister of the Dead (Friars' Cemetery)
G. Cemetery of the Avelli

Masaccio: The most holy Trinity, detail.

Domenico Ghirlanduio: The nativity of S. John the Baptist.

Andrea di Bonaiuto: Allegory of the Church - The Capital Vices, detail.

In the *Sacristy* nearby there is a *Crucifixion* by **Maso di Bartolomeo** (15th c.), a *wash-basin* in marble and polychrome terracotta by **Giovanni della Robbia** (1498) and, in the left nave, the well-known fresco of the *Trinity* by **Masaccio** (circa 1427) which presents a painted version of the Renaissance architectural values of space.

Finally, in the *Green Cloister* inside the monumental area, beside the church, is the *Great Spanish Chapel*, built by **Jacopo Talenti** after 1350 and decorated inside with frescoes by **Andrea da Firenze** and his assistants around 1355; in the *Refectory* the remains of the detached frescoes by **Paolo Uccello,** which once decorated the lunettes in the cloister, can be seen.

Botticelli: Nativity, detail.

3 **CENACLE OF FOLIGNO** (42, via Faenza) - On the wall at the back of the ancient refectory of the ex Convent of St Onofrio, run by the Franciscan nuns "of Foligno", is a *fresco* of the *Last Supper*. When it was discovered in 1845 it was attributed to Raphael; today it is thought to be a work of **Perugino** painted around 1490. The iconography is typical of Florentine Cenacles of the late Renaissance, enriched however by the background of characteristic Umbrian scenery in which the Prayer in the Garden is set.

4 **OGNISSANTI CHURCH AND CENACLE** (42, Borgo Ognissanti) - Built in 1251, it was completely rebuilt by **Bartolomeo Pettirossi** in 1627. The baroque *façade*, decorated in terracotta, is by **Matteo Negetti** (1637). The fine thirteenth-century *bell tower* is all that remains of the original structure.

The *interior*, one nave with transept, was decorated almost entirely during the baroque period.

On the second altar on the right is the *Madonna of Mercy* and below the *Pietà* frescoed by **Domenico** and **Davide del Ghirlandaio**; at the foot of the altar is a tomb-stone of the Vespucci family. Between the third and fourth altars is the famous fresco by **Botticelli**, *St Augustin in his Study* (1480) and opposite, on the left wall, *St Jerome in his Study*, by **Ghirlandaio**, both restored. In the *Sacristy*: *Crucifix* painted on wood by the school of Giotto and *frescoes* by **Agnolo** and **Taddeo Gaddi**.

After being restored, the seventeenth-century lunette frescoes depicting scenes from the life of St Francis, have been placed in the adjacent *cloisters*, and clearly demonstrate the elegance of Michelozzi's style. From here one accedes to the *Last Supper* in the ancient refectory of the convent next to the church, painted by **Domenico del Ghirlandaio** in 1480. There are also some detached frescoes and sinopias which form a small museum.

Domenico Ghirlandaio: The last Supper, detail.

CORSINI PALACE AND GALLERY (10, Lungarno Corsini) - Built in 1648-56 by the architects **Silvani** and **Ferri**, it retains a sixteenth-century lay-out but is decorated in baroque style. The *Gallery* is situated on the first floor and is one of the most important private collections in Florence. Begun in 1765 by Lorenzo Corsini, it houses Florentine works of the fifteenth and sixteenth centuries and others of the seventeenth century Italian and foreign schools. Amongst the most important are: *Apollo and the Muses* by **Timoteo Viti**, *Madonna with Child and St John* by **Pontormo**, *Madonna and Saints* by **Signorelli** and a *Crucifixion* attributed to **Antonello da Messina.**

To the right of the Palace is the *Ponte alla Carraia*. The bridge was built in 1220 and destroyed by the flood in 1333. It was rebuilt in 1346. Like the other bridges in Florence it was rebuilt after the war in its old form.

Proceeding along Lungarno Corsini one comes to *Ponte Santa Trinita*, rebuilt by **Ammannati** in 1567-70 on the site of the thirteenth-century wooden bridge, following suggestions by Michelangelo.

During the Second World War it was completely destroyed and then rebuilt to the sixteenth-century original design using all the material it was possible to recover.

From this bridge one arrives in *via Tornabuoni*, an elegant Florentine street lined with impressive buildings, to name but two: the *Spini-Feroni Palace* (late thirteenth century), the *Bartolini Salimbeni Palace*, a work by **Baccio d'Agnolo** who, with this building gave new impetus to civil building in the sixteenth century.

At the end of the street one comes to the *Antinori Palace* (1461-66) and the *Church of St Gaetano*, a rare example of baroque architecture in Florence, rebuilt by **Nigetti** and **Silvani** during the seventeenth century.

5

6 **BASILICA OF SANTA TRINITA** (piazza Santa Trinita) - Built in the eleventh century in Romanesque style by the Vallombrosian monks, this church was transformed and enlarged in the thirteenth and fourteenth centuries to its present form. The *façade* is attributed to **Bernardo Buontalenti** (1594). The **interior**, shaped like an Egyptian cross, is one of the finest examples of Florentine Gothic style. In the *Sassetti Chapel* is the famous series of frescoes depicting the *Life of St Francis*, painted by **Domenico del Ghirlandaio** between 1483 and 1486. In the fourth chapel to the right there are frescoes and a painting of the *Annunciation* by **Lorenzo Monaco**.

D. Ghirlandaio: Basilica of S. Trinità - Sassetti Chapel, The Adoration of the Shepherds.

7 **CHURCH OF THE SANTI APOSTOLI** (1, piazza del Limbo) - Built at the end of the eleventh century on the remains of ancient Roman baths, it keeps to the primitive basilica structure and represents the prototype of Florentine Romanesque churches. It was restored several times during the fifteenth and sixteenth centuries. The fine sixteenth-century *portal* is attributed to **Benedetto da Rovezzano**. The *interior* is full of priceless works including the *Immaculate Conception* by **Vasari**, the polychrome clay *Tabernacle* by **Andrea della Robbia** and the *Funeral monument to Oddo Altoviti* by **Benedetto da Rovezzano**.

8 **PARTE GUELFA PALACE** (piazza di Parte Guelfa) - The modifications in style that took place from the fourteenth to the sixteenth century can be clearly seen in this palace, which was begun in the early fourteenth century and enlarged in the fifteenth and sixteenth centuries. It still has the beautiful Brunelleschi *hall* with its wooden ceiling by **Vasari** and a terracotta *lunette* by **Luca della Robbia,** the elegant *little loggia* is also by **Vasari**.

DAVANZATI PALACE (9, via Porta Rossa) - An aristocratic palace, built around the middle of the fourteenth century although the upper loggia is a fifteenth-century addition. **9**

It now houses the *Museum of the Antica Casa Fiorentina* (Museum of the Old Florentine House) and gives a very good insight into the furnishing of private homes in the fifteenth and sixteenth centuries. The exhibits consist of furniture, ceramics, paintings, sculptures, tapestries and objects for domestic use. An array of *coats-of-arms* decorate the walls, especially in the Peacock Room on the first floor. In the square below is the *Foresi family tower-house*, one of the few remaining in this district, bearing witness to the popularity of these buildings in Medieval Florence.

STROZZI PALACE (piazza Strozzi) - Considered the finest Florentine palace of the Renaissance period. Begun by **Benedetto da Maiano** in 1489, it was continued by **Simone del Pollaiolo**, known as Cronaca, until 1504, when building was interrupted before the back was completed. **10**

The palace has three floors and is in rustic ashlar work, decorated with twin-light mullioned windows and crowned by a huge cornice which stands out against another smooth wide fascia, separating it from the rest of the building. Today it is the headquarters of important cultural institutes and periodically houses important exhibitions.

RUCELLAI LOGGIA AND PALACE (18, via della Vigna Nuova) - Built by **Bernardo Rossellino** (1446-51) to a design by **Alberti**, it is the first Palace in which the Brunelleschi style is abandoned and the Roman style of dividing a building into three architectonic orders, one above the other, is adopted. **11**

Opposite the palace is the *Loggia dei Rucellai* (1460-66). From the fourteenth century a loggia was a typical addition to great Florentine palaces where the owners held banquets and meetings.

FRATELLI ALINARI MUSEUM OF THE HISTORY OF PHOTO-GRAPHY (Largo Alinari, 15) - **12**

Opened in 1985, it exhibits the photographic archives of the *Alinari Brothers*, the oldest firm of photographers, with the addition of several other Italian and foreign collections. Particularly noteworthy is the collection of cameras, lenses and antique objects used in photography.

The Museum also has an interesting programme of periodic, historic and monographic exhibitions.

MARINO MARINI MUSEUM (piazza di S. Pancrazio) - In the ancient church of *St Pancreas*, which was converted by interesting architectural redesign work in 1988, 176 sculptures, paintings and drawings by **Marino Marini** (1901-1980) have been collected, donated by the artist to the city of Florence, including some of his famous "*Cavalieri*" and *Pomone*. **13**

RUCELLAI CHAPEL (via della Spada) - Next to the former church of St Pancreas, in the *Rucellai Chapel* (visits by request, with entrance from via della Spada) is the extremely elegant *church of Santo Sepolcro,* a true marble jewel of Albertian architecture (1467). **14**

SEVENTH ITINERARY
I-OUTSIDE THE CITY WALLS

OUTSIDE THE CITY WALLS - Over the centuries, like all Medieval cities, Florence has several times extended the perimeter of its outer walls; on the third and most important occasion they were designed by Arnolfo di Cambio and completed in 1229. After the unity of Italy, the walls were destroyed in order to give more space to the city, and wide avenues were built by the architect **Giuseppe Poggi**, who took great care to save the main city gates from demolition; it is therefore still possible to admire, in the centre of vast squares, *Porta al Prato, Porta San Gallo, Porta alla Croce, Porta San Niccolò, Porta San Frediano* and *Porta Romana.*

1 FORTEZZA DA BASSO - (Fortress) Built by **Antonio San Gallo** between 1533 and 1535 to provide the city with military protection. Today it is the headquarters of the *Chamber of Art Restoration*, the most important in Italy together with the one in Rome, and a centre for exhibitions and trade fairs.

2 PALAZZO DEI CONGRESSI (Conference Hall Palace) (2, viale Filippo Strozzi) Opposite the Fortress, on the same side as the walls, is the Palazzo dei Congressi. Designed by the architect Spadolini in the park of *Villa Vittoria,* formerly Strozzi-Ridolfi, who, with brilliant modern architectural work has combined utility with respect for the surrounding environment.
Near the Fortezza da Basso, along Viale Milton, is the *Russian Orthodox Church.*

3 RUSSIAN ORTHODOX CHURCH (8, via Leone X) - This church was built from 1899 to 1903 by the architect **Preobragenski** in the style of Russian churches for the Orthodox community in Florence, today reduced to just a few members. The iconostasis, which still today adorns the church, was donated by Tsar Nicholas II.
Proceeding along the Ring Avenues (Viali di Circonvallazione), one comes to *Piazza della Libertà*, designed at the end of the nineteenth century by **Poggi**, based on Florentine Renaissance style. In the centre of the Piazza is the *Porta San Gallo* (1284) and the great *Arch of Triumph* erected for the entrance of Francis II of Lorraine as successor to the Medicis (1739). From here, returning up the Montughi hill, one arrives at the nineteenth-century *Villa Stibbert*, which today houses the Museum of the same name.

4 STIBBERT MUSEUM (1, via Stibbert) - This Museum exhibits paintings (**Crivelli, Tiepolo**) cloths, furniture and porcelain, but

Russian-Orthodox Church.

above all, arms, which Frederick Stibbert, an Englishman, collected during his life-time. His aim was to recreate the atmosphere of past ages and in this he succeeded, especially with the Procession of Knights and Foot Soldiers, in Italian, Spanish, German and Saracen armour of the sixteenth century.

ENGLISH CEMETERY - Situated in the centre of Piazzale **5** Donatello and surrounded by splendid cypress trees. Among those buried here are the poetess Elizabeth Barrett Browning, the poet Arthur Clough, the writer Frances Milton Trollope, the preacher Theodore Parker and Giovanni Pietro Vieusseux, one of the protagonists of literary and political culture in nineteenth-century Florence. This characteristic cemetery inspired Arnold Böcklin to paint his well-known picture *The Isle of the Dead*.

SAN SALVI ABBEY (16, via San Salvi) - Built in the eleventh **6** century by the Vallombrosian monks, it was almost completely destroyed during the siege of 1312 and then rebuilt and renovated in later years. The ***Church of St Michael*** and the ***Convent*** are part of this Abbey where, besides the collection of *altar-pieces* from the

103

sixteenth and seventeenth-century Florentine school (Vasari, Gabbiani, M. Rosselli), and some pieces by Bertolini, of particular interest is the *Refectory* frescoed by **Andrea del Sarto** and his school (Puligo, Sogliani). On the central wall is the *Last Supper* (1519) which, with its harmony of space, sense of colour and elegant drawing, can be considered his masterpiece.

7 STATE ARCHIVES - (viale Giovane Italia) Returning to the ring avenues, near the ancient *Porta alla Croce* (1284) in the centre of piazza Beccaria stands the modern *State Archives* building where scholars may consult the important and abundant documentation preserved in the various archives of lay and religious institutions from the eighth century onwards, including those of the ancient Florentine Republic, the Medici and Lorraine Archives and those of the numerous convents and charity institutes which were closed in 1809. After reaching the Lungarno (Arno Embankment), crossing *Ponte S. Niccolo* and proceeding along the panoramic *Viale dei Colli*, which, like the other avenues, was designed by **Giuseppe Poggi** (1865-70), one arrives at *Michelangelo Square.*

8 MICHELANGELO SQUARE (piazzale Michelangelo)- A wide terrace from where it is possible to admire one of the most superb views of the city nestling in the Arno valley, surrounded by gently sloping hills. In the centre of the square stands the *Monument to Michelangelo* (1875) with a bronze reproduction of the four statues depicting Day, Night, Dawn and Dusk, dominated by the statue of David. On the hill behind Piazzale Michelangelo stands the *Church of San Miniato al Monte.*

Panorama of Florence from Piazzale Michelangelo.

9 CHURCH OF SAN MINIATO AL MONTE - Rebuilt after 1018 on the site of an existing church, it is one of the finest examples of Florentine Romanesque style. The twelfth and thirteenth-century *façade* is covered with green and white marble to create geometrical figures and is in two layers: the lower part consists of five arches with five portals, three of which open; the remaining two (the second and the fourth) are false, but the polychrome decorations

View of the Church of San Miniato al Monte.

Interior of the Church of San Miniato al Monte.

create an admirable optical effect so that they appear to be real doors. The top part, which is only over the central door, is decorated with a thirteenth-century mosaic of *Christ giving his blessing.*

The *interior* is divided into a nave and two aisles by clustered columns and pilasters with a polychrome beamed roof. The nave retains its original marble decorations and ends in a crypt dominated by an *apse* with five arches repeating the architectural motive of the façade. Alone, in front of the *crypt* stands the *Crucifix Chapel* by **Michelozzo**, shaped like a shrine and decorated with a *coffered ceiling* in glazed terracotta by **Luca della Robbia** (1448).

The *Sacristy* is completely covered with frescoes by **Spinello Aretino** depicting *Stories of St Benedict* (1387).

Mosaic: Jesus Christ, the Virgin and Saint Miniato.

In the *left nave* is the **Chapel of the Cardinal of Portugal**, so called because of the *tomb* that **Antonio Rossellino** had sculptured for him. It was built by **Manetti** in 1461-1466. The vault of the chapel is decorated by five glazed terracotta *roundels* by **Luca della Robbia.** Continuing along Viale dei Colli one comes to *Via San Leonardo*, a picturesque little street on a hillside, which leads to *Forte Belvedere*.

10 **FORTE BELVEDERE** - A splendid example of a military fortress, overlooking *Boboli Gardens*. It was built in the sixteenth century by **Bernardo Buontalenti,** commissioned by Grand Duke Ferdinand I. Today this austere fortress is frequently the venue of exhibitions and cultural events. A superb view of the city can be enjoyed from this terrace.
Returning to Viale dei Colli and continuing along the same road, one comes to *Porta Romana* (1326). By crossing Viale Petrarca one reaches *Porta San Frediano* (1334) and from this road, continuing along Via Pisana, one can climb up to *Monte Oliveto* and the *Bellosguardo Hill*, areas abounding in historical and literary memories and ancient monuments; they offer a splendid view of the city and the unspoilt Tuscan countryside with its softly undulating hills covered with cypress and olive trees.
Returning down towards the city, across the *Ponte della Vittoria,* rebuilt after the last war, one comes to the *Cascine Park.*

11 **CASCINE PARK** - This is a splendid and immense public park, once a farmstead of the Grand Dukes. It extends for over 3 km. to the west of the city on the right bank of the River Arno up to its confluence with the Mugnone river and is a favourite walk of the Florentines. Many avenues and paths intertwine among the vast areas of luxuriant vegetation. At the end of the park, which caters for a wide range of sports (horse-racing, tennis courts, swimming pools), is a *monument* to the Indian Prince Rajaram Cuttraputti (1874) who died in Florence at the age of 20 and was cremated here in accordance with Hindu custom. Leaving the Park and passing the *Porta al Prato* (1284), one returns to the Fortezza da Basso.

SURROUNDING DISTRICTS

FIESOLE - This little town stands on a hill overlooking the Arno **1**
and Mugnone valleys; it was once an important Etruscan, Roman
and Medieval city but following the rise of Florence to supremacy its
importance began to decline in the twelfth century; it was however
given a new lease of life in the fifteenth century due to the
generous help of the Medici family and the outstanding work of its
artists.

CONVENT OF SAN DOMENICO (piazza San Domenico) - The **2**
convent was built in the fifteenth century and restored in the
seventeenth century by **Nigetti** to whom we also owe the beautiful
Bell Tower and the *Church* with its porticoed *façade.* St Antonino and
Beato Angelico, who was also the Prior of the Convent, lived here.
By Frá Angelico one can admire: The *Madonna with Angels and
Saints* in the Church and a fresco depicting the *Crucifixion* in the
Chapter House.

BADIA FIESOLANA (via Badia dei Roccettini) - This austere and **3**
huge Church, built in the early Middle Ages, was the Fiesole
Cathedral until 1026. It was home of the Camaldolensian Monks,
then the Benedictines and finally the Canons of the first Order of St
Augustine. Rebuilding began in 1456, thanks to the generosity of
Cosimo the Elder, but on his death in 1464, the lower part of the
XII century Romanesque *façade* in white and green marble was left
unfinished. The harmonious *interior* is reminiscent of Brunelleschi
architecture and the nave has side chapels decorated with sixteenth-
century altars. The adjoining ex-convent in which Cosimo the Elder
collected manuscripts and rare books was in 1753 the home of the
"Accademia dei Georgofili" (Agrarians), but now houses the
European University.

Badia fiesolana.

107

Aerial view of Fiesole.

4 **CATHEDRAL** - Dedicated to St Romolo it was built in 1028 and subsequently enlarged. Further alterations were made in the nineteenth century. The Romanesque **Bell Tower** (1217) has a crenellated top. The *interior* has three naves and, like the Church of San Miniato al Monte, the apse is raised over the crypt. The **Salutati Chapel** in the presbytery houses the *tomb of Bishop Leonardo Salutati*, a notable work of **Mino da Fiesole.**
In front of the Duomo, overlooking the characteristic Square is the **Seminary** (1697) and on its right the **Bishop's Palace** founded in the eleventh century and rebuilt in the seventeenth century.

5 **CONVENT OF SAN FRANCESCO** - On the highest point of the hill (Etruscan-Roman acropolis), stands the Convent of St. Francis. From here (**Belvedere**) there is a splendid view of the vast Arno Valley and the city of Florence.
The Convent was built as an Oratory for the Florentine Hermits in 1330 and rebuilt by the Franciscan Monks in 1407. The little church, with its Gothic interior, preserves a *Crucifixion* by **Neri di Bicci**, *Madonna and Saints* by **Perugino**, a beautiful *Annunciation* by **Raffaellino del Garbo** and a sixteenth-century inlaid *choir-stall*. Going down from the Sacristy Cloister one reaches the **Missionary Ethnographic Museum**, which has an Etruscan, Roman and, a more important Chinese section. Adjoining the church is the pretty little XVI century cloister, dedicated to St Bernardino da Siena.

6 **ROMAN THEATRE** (1, via Marini) - Built during the time of Silla and embellished by Claudius and Septimus Severus, it holds 3,000 people and has an auditorium with three tiers of seats and nineteen steps. The adjoining **Archaeological Museum** preserves Hellenistic

Fiesole: Cathedral.

and Roman finds from the theatre and the area surrounding Ficsole.

BANDINI MUSEUM (1, via Duprè) - Opened to the public in 1878, it houses mainly paintings and sculptures by the fourteenth and fifteenth-century Florentine school; amongst these there are works by: **A. Gaddi, L. Monaco,** and **Iacopo del Sellaio.** Of particular interest, on the ground floor, is the collection of *Robbian terracottas.* **7**

DUPRE' MUSEUM (19, Via Duprè) - From the Cathedral square, turning into Via Duprè, in a suggestive position, is the tiny *Duprè Museum,* which houses almost all the plaster works made by this sculptor and which has recently been donated to the town by the artist's heirs. **8**

SETTIGNANO - A beautiful hillside area just outside Florence and the birthplace of numerous artists (Desiderio da Settignano, the Rossellinos, Luca Fancelli). Its splendid woodlands and monuments make it an ideal place for interesting walks. Among its various monuments are: the Romanesque *Church of St Martino a Mensola*, the fifteenth-century *Church of the Assumption, Castello di Vincigliata*, with its crenellated tower, *Villa Gamberaia*, with its sixteenth-century Italian landscape garden, and *Villa i Tatti*, which houses the *Berenson Library and Collection*, with works by **Giotto, B. Daddi, G. da Milano, S. Martini, P. Lorenzetti. D. Veneziano, L. Signorelli, G. Bellini, V. Foppa** and **Cima da Conegliano.** **9**

CERTOSA MONASTERY OF GALLUZZO (Carthusian Monastery) - A monumental group of buildings built in 1341, later enlarged **10**

and restored, so that now all kinds of styles, ranging from Gothic to neo-classical, can be seen in the architecture and decoration. From the entrance staircase one enters the *Art Gallery* which houses, among other works, five frescoed *lunettes,* in very poor condition, of the *Passion cycle* by **Pontormo** (1525), recently detached from the large cloister.

The *Church*, with its sixteenth-century façade and large rectangular courtyard in front, is dedicated to San Lorenzo and houses a wooden inlaid choir-stall and paintings by **Poccetti, Giovanni** and **Rutilio Manetti**. Also worth a visit are the monks' *cells* which look out over the suggestive and imposing *Cloister*.

The Carthusian Monastery of Galluzzo, general view.

11 **MEDICEAN VILLAS** - Many villas were built following the rise to power of the Medici family and consequent foundation of the Grand-Duchy of Tuscany and also as a result of the family's policy of investing in land and buildings which led to extension of estates already in their possession as well as others newly acquired by various means, including confiscation.

Villa di Careggi (Florence) - Rebuilt and fortified by **Michelozzo** (1433), it was the residence, together with other members of the family, of Lorenzo the Magnificent, who set up a kind of literary circle there (Accademia Platonica). It has frescoes by **Pontormo** and **Bronzino**.

Villa di Castello (in the locality of Castello, 6 km. north-west of Florence) - A thirteenth-century villa restored around 1480 by **Vasari** and frescoed by **Pontormo** and **Volterrano**. Giovanni delle Bande Nere grew up here and today it is the headquarters, *Library* and *Museum* of the *Accademia della Crusca*. The outstanding sixteenth-century park, designed by **Niccolò Tribolo**, is decorated with sculptures by **Ammannati** and **Giambologna.**

Villa la Petraia (in the locality of Castello) - Once a medieval Castle, it was rebuilt by **Bernardo Buontalenti** (1575) and later frescoed by **Volterrano** with the apotheosis and portraits of the Medici family. It had a moment of glory in the nineteenth century when it became the Summer Residence of the Savoys, the ruling monarchs; its Park merges with that of Villa di Castello.

Villa di Poggio a Caiano (18 km west of Florence) - Begun in 1480 by **Giuliano da Sangallo**, it was continued by **Buontalenti**. It was the favourite residence of the Medici family from Lorenzo the

Magnificent to Prince Ferdinand and later of Victor Emmanuel II of Savoy who lived there with his "Bella Rosina" (Countess of Mirafiori).
Immortalised by poets like **Crespi** (*The Fair at Poggio a Caiano*), it is embellished with Robbian terracottas and works by **B. Bandinelli, Franciabigio, Pontormo** (*Allegory of Vertunno and Pomona*), **A. Allori** and **Andrea del Sarto**.

Villa di Artimino (22 km west of Florence) - Built by **Buontalenti** in 1594, it was ideally situated in the centre of the Medici estates and represented a synthesis of the family's economic and political power.
From the top of a hill it overlooks the vast panorama of the Arno Valley from Florence to Prato and Pistoia and is considered one of the most outstanding Medicean villas. The characteristic *village* of *Artimino, in front of the Villa and still surrounded by medieval walls, is of great interest.*

Villa Belcanto (Fiesole) - Very little remains (the hanging garden) of the building erected by **Michelozzo** in 1458 for Cosimo the Elder. During Lorenzo the Magnificent's time, personages such as Poliziano and Pico della Mirandola stayed there.

CHURCH OF ST JOHN THE BAPTIST (Autostrada del Sole - Florence North exit) - Built by **Giovanni Michelucci** between 1961 and 1968, it is one of the most unusual and representative examples of post-war rationalist architecture. **12**
The general structure resembles a tent, giving those travelling along the motorway the feeling of "transit" and a restful meditative interlude. Of the many elements that go into the significance of this complex work, of particular interest are the *panels* by **Emilio Greco** depicting the patron saints of the main cities through which the motorway passes.
Michelucci also designed the Florence *Santa Maria Novella railway station*, again adopting forms and materials borrowed from tradition but used in modern key to create a harmonious and significant setting.

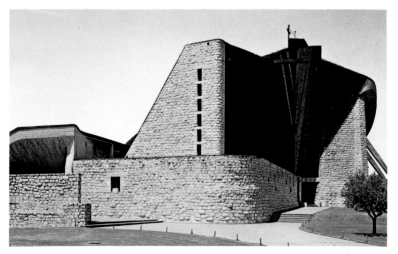

Church of St John the Baptist.

INDEX

© ATS Italia Editrice s.r.l.
Made in Italy
www.atsitalia.it
sede di Roma:
via di Brava, 41/43
tel. 06 66415961
e-mail: atsitalia@atsitalia.it
sede di Firenze:
largo Liverani, 12/3
tel.055 4220577
e-mail: becoccieditore@atsitalia.it

Il marchio **B**
è un marchio ATS Italia Editrice

Photographies:
Casa Editrice Giusti
of S. Becocci and C. - Florence
Sovrintendenza ai Beni
Ambientali e
Architettonici, restoration
of The last Judgement,
detail; p. 46
Arte e Immagine S.R.L.
Text:
Giovanni Casetta
*Graphic Design
and pagination:*
Carlo Mannucci
Cover:
Massimo Capaccioli
Editing:
Casa Editrice Giusti of S. Becocci

Printing:
Graficalito Firenze